Germany's

's

30 Years After R

KEITH FENDER

THE WORLD'S RAILWAYS SERIES, VOLUME 3

Front cover image: DB's latest ICE 4 high-speed train is seen at the rebuilt Erfurt Hauptbahnhof station on 28 February 2020 with a Berlin to Munich service. The Italianate tower on the left of the picture is part of the original station and dates from 1846.

Back cover image: The sun sets at Schwandorf on 27 May 1999 as Soviet-built diesel loco 234 548 waits to leave with InterRegio service IR 2069 to Chemnitz.

Title page image: The railway in transition at Eisleben in central Germany in May 1999 as an ICE high-speed train speeds past a Class 772 railcar waiting to work a rural passenger train. All of the three branch lines that once radiated from Eisleben have since closed and been lifted.

Contents page image: DB's largest class of diesel locomotives, Class 218, is rapidly being replaced by new multiple units or electrification. In the last summer of operation before replacement by new DMUs on the route, 218 420 is seen near its destination of Füssen in the Bavarian Alps with a service from Munich on 27 September 2018.

Acknowledgements

Thanks are due to multiple companies and individuals for their assistance over the years and with information for this book, especially Deutsche Bahn, Keolis, RDC Deutschland, Siemens, Bombardier and Alstom. All pictures are by the author except where stated. My thanks to Andrew Garrett, Jon Hayes, Jim Rose and Deutsche Bahn AG for the use of their pictures where shown. Special thanks to Sue for many years of enjoying multiple visits to Germany.

References

The UK magazines Modern Railways and Today's Railways Europe have both offered good coverage in English of German railway operations during the last three decades. In addition, the German language magazines Bahn Report and Drehschiebe are highly recommended.

Large amounts of publicly available information from DB, Siemens, Bombardier, the German Federal statistical service Destatis, the Federal Railway Office (Eisenbahnamt) and the European Commission have also been used to prepare this book.

For detailed fleet information in English, the German Railways Handbooks produced by Platform 5 Publishing are recommended. For a detailed German railway atlas, the Eisenbahnatlas Deutschland, published by Verlag Schweers und Wall, is also highly recommended.

Published by Key Books
An imprint of Key Publishing Ltd
PO Box 100
Stamford
Lincs PE19 1XQ

www.keypublishing.com

ISBN 978 1 913870 06 5

Typeset by SJmagic DESIGN SERVICES, India.

Contents

Chapter 1

Introduction and Historical Overview

Germany's railway system is one of the largest and most advanced in the world. This book aims to show how the railway network has changed and adapted since Germany was re-unified as a single country on 3 October, 1990, after 45 years of post-World War Two division.

Just as the country itself has changed significantly as a result, the railway industry has altered almost beyond recognition. In 1990, the two state-owned railway operators largely monopolised their industry in the two halves of Germany while, 30 years later, there are over 440 rail operators and around 175 companies managing parts of the railway network!

New high-speed lines have been built, enabling journeys between major cities that are competitive with flying, and ambitious plans have been announced to introduce significantly more high-speed connections operating every half an hour on all major routes by 2030.

Divided Country

At the end of World War Two in May 1945, Germany was occupied by the armies of the Allies, who had pre-agreed geographical zones for each major power to administer. In the west of the country, the British occupied the north of Germany with the USA taking much of the south, except the south-western part of the country which was occupied by the French Army. In the east of Germany, the Soviet Red Army occupied around a third of the country which included Berlin; although the capital was itself sub-divided into four zones, each administered by one of the occupying powers.

Germany's eastern borders also moved westwards in 1945 with Poland gaining a swathe of territory that included major German cities such as Breslau (now Wrocław). This was designed to compensate Poland for losing significant territory in the east, which was incorporated into the USSR under plans agreed by Soviet leader Josef Stalin with UK Prime Minister Winston Churchill and US Presidents Roosevelt and Truman at the Yalta and Potsdam conferences in 1945.

Most German cities were in ruins as were large parts of the rail network. Allied air raids had deliberately targeted entire cities with important war industries and railway junctions, yards and depots were high on that target list. Within a few years, reconstruction work re-opened much of the rail network and repaired much of the damaged rolling stock, although the approach taken varied depending upon which occupation zone the railway was in.

The western powers relatively quickly decided to restart the German economy to provide jobs and food for the population whereas, in the Soviet occupied zone, recovery of equipment and machinery that could be of value in reconstructing the war ravaged Soviet Union (USSR) was the highest priority in 1945-46. Large parts of the eastern rail network were used as a source of parts to rebuild Soviet railways with double track lines reduced to single track, while overhead electrification and locomotives, both steam and electric, were taken as war reparations.

Within two years, a new geopolitical power struggle began between the communist Soviet Union and the western powers, now known as the Cold War. This led to the formal division of Germany into two separate countries; West Germany (or Bundesrepublik Deutschland) with its capital in Bonn beside the

River Rhine, and East Germany which was officially known as the Deutsche Demokratische Republik (German Democratic Republic) or DDR, which we will use in this book. West Germany was founded in 1949 with its constitution known as the Basic Law; it explicitly allowed for re-unification of the whole country at some unknown point in the future.

In the DDR, the state railway adopted the same name as the pre-war operator Deutsche Reichsbahn (DR) while in West Germany, the name was changed to Deutsche Bundesbahn, meaning federal (Bund) railway (bahn). Berlin was also divided into West Berlin, which was surrounded on all sides by the DDR, and East Berlin, which was the DDR's capital.

Thanks to wartime agreements between the Allies, trains, flights and road access across the DDR were guaranteed for the western armies, although not for German civilians. An early attempt by the Soviet forces and DDR authorities to shut Berlin off from the western powers was defeated through the operation of the Berlin airlift from western Germany for nearly a year in 1948-49, which ended up bringing in not only food but even coal!

The DDR became the most loyal of all the eastern bloc Soviet satellite states, initially to Stalin and then later leaders. Despite its official name, the DDR was no democracy but a one party state and rapidly started to lose people, often the highly skilled or better educated, to West Germany. While the border between east and west in the countryside was fairly well guarded, in Berlin you could move from one part of the city to another on the S-Bahn or U-Bahn train and, once in West Berlin, refugees from the DDR were given jobs, flats and allowances.

Despite increased controls, the flow of people continued so, with little warning, the DDR built a wall around West Berlin in August 1961. This barrier, initially built out of cement blocks and barbed wire, became one of the most complex border structures in history and rapidly acquired notoriety as East German border guards followed orders to shoot to kill anyone trying to flee the country.

The Berlin Wall, as it was known in English, became the symbol of the Cold War with American presidents visiting Berlin and demanding its removal. The wall was officially called the Anti-Fascist Protection Wall or Antifaschistischer Schutzwall by the East German government, which attempted to explain it as a protective measure to an increasingly unconvinced population who were prohibited to travel to the west.

While the western powers objected noisily to the Berlin Wall, little actually changed for many years and West Germany went from strength to strength in a period known as the Wirtschaftswunder (Economic Wonder) between the 1950s and 1970s, aided initially by Marshall Plan loans from the USA.

In contrast, the DDR stagnated, even though it was nominally more prosperous than most of its fellow socialist countries and much better off than its Soviet guarantor. Heavy industry was re-established in the 1950s; this including major rail engineering factories that would build locomotives for export all over the eastern bloc Comecon trading area. The DDR was of great strategic importance to the USSR as a base for hundreds of thousands of Red Army troops close to the borders with NATO member West Germany. It was also crucial as a source of uranium, which was mined near Dresden and Gera and used in Soviet nuclear weapons.

In the end, creeping political freedom in Poland and Hungary in the 1980s along with changes in the Soviet leadership and the new approach of Glasnost or openness proposed by new Soviet leader Mikhail Gorbachev spelt the end for the DDR, although it was not immediately obvious how the endgame would play out.

Weekly demonstrations in major East German cities, especially Leipzig, from September 1989 were filmed and then screened on West German television. Despite watching it being technically illegal, almost everyone in the DDR did as well (the transmitters in West Germany were deliberately powerful so as to reach almost all of the DDR) so people became aware of the protests and the numbers attending increased. Unable to rely on Soviet military assistance, or even its own secret police, to quell the protests as had happened before, the East German government changed leadership in October 1989.

Unexpectedly, the East German government announced on 9 November 1989 that travel to West Germany, banned since 1961, was now possible and immediately. Once the first border crossings had let hundreds leave East Berlin, there was no going back and within weeks of 'die Wende' ('the turn' as this moment is referred to in German), full re-unification of the two countries was under discussion. The first and only democratic election in the DDR's history in March 1990 produced strong support for West German Chancellor Helmut Kohl's Christian Democrat (CDU) party and rapid re-unification.

Events then moved quicker than most people expected with monetary, economic and social union occurring on 1 July 1990. This had the effect of treating the East German currency as equivalent to the West German Deutschemark, the Ost Mark as it was termed had previously been almost worthless outside the DDR. While this move may have won votes and provided East German families with windfall Deutschmark cash, it sealed the fate of many East German companies as they were no longer guaranteed sales in the Comecon bloc. They were also unable to compete with West German companies when suddenly paying similar wages and charging similar prices.

After votes by the parliaments of both countries, the DDR formally joined West Germany, meaning that from re-unification day on 3 October 1990, East German citizens were now members of the European Union and NATO, despite their country still being home to thousands of Soviet soldiers. The latter would all eventually leave by 1994, returning mostly to Russia as the USSR had also ceased to exist by then.

The brutal reality of a divided country, this being the view from a train crossing into East Berlin on the Berlin Stadtbahn in August 1981. The train has just passed over the border and the outer Berlin Wall; the wide expanse of open ground with fences and obstacles was designed to enable border guards to be able to spot anybody attempting to cross it. The railway viaduct formed part of the inner wall which can then be seen on the left, this was painted white. (Jim Rose)

Almost exactly the same spot in the 21st century as the new Berlin Hauptbahnhof station is built metres from the former wall. A train to Stuttgart operated by short-lived open access private operator Locomore is seen arriving at Berlin Hbf on 31 March 2017 hauled by Swedish-registered Eurosprinter loco 242 517 (182 517). The gabled brick-built building visible on the right above the rear of the train is the Charitié Hospital; in the 1981 picture (above) the hospital is just visible on the extreme left above the train.

Soviet Red Army soldiers boarding a one-coach troop train at Leipzig Hbf on 29 March 1991. The train is DR two-axle railcar 171 034. Later reclassified as Class 771/772 by DB, these units were known as Ferkeltaxis in the DDR, so nicknamed as farmers in rural areas used them to take small animals including piglets (Ferkel) to market!

The transition from a planned economy and police state to being part of Europe's largest democratic country was traumatic and expensive. Taxes on West Germans were increased to fund solidarity payments to help rebuild the East. Many in the former DDR lost their jobs as once apparently successful companies failed or were privatised, being unable to compete with western prices or technology. Initially, prices and wages in the east were lower but over time have largely levelled up. Some, mainly older, former citizens of the DDR still hark back to simpler and more certain times, but surveys show few want to actually turn the clock back, even if that were possible.

Huge amounts of public investment in everything from water supplies to transport infrastructure started to change the economy in the 1990s and, 30 years on, some eastern cities are now seeing their populations expanding with successful new industries and universities along with tourism all contributing to make the united Germany Europe's largest economy.

The first 30 years after re-unification would see major changes as all of the DDR's former allies also got rid of communist rule, with almost all of them joining the EU by 2007. The united Germany became a major driver for closer European integration within the European Union and was a key backer of the Euro single currency introduced in 1999; the new European Central Bank which oversees the Euro is based in Frankfurt am Main.

The Eurozone and European Single Market coupled with increasing globalisation, which saw production outsourced to Asian countries, has led to a boom in container shipping which has in turn led to much more intermodal freight on Europe's railways. This is particularly true in Germany, which now handles thousands of containers each month delivered from China both by sea or by rail via Russia.

The railways of the newly re-unified Germany in 1990 included some locomotives that dated back to the pre-1945 state railway. DR electric loco 254 106, seen at Leipzig Engelsdorf shed on 29 March 1991, was delivered by AEG as E94 106 in September 1943 and initially used on the electrified line between Leipzig and Nuremberg. The loco, along with many others in the Soviet-occupied zone, was taken to the Soviet Union in 1946 and used to operate a freight line at Vorkuta in northern Russia, this using overhead line equipment also removed from eastern Germany by the Red Army. The loco along with 28 sisters was returned to the DDR in 1952; the majority were eventually overhauled and used on lines that were re-electrified by DR. 254 106 was stored by the company just before re-unification but used for a farewell special in December 1990 and not officially withdrawn until 31 January 1992. Today, it is preserved at the railway museum in Weimar.

While DR had 'officially' stopped using steam locos in May 1988, there were a small number still in operational condition in 1990 and a larger number in use as stationary steam generators (Dampfspender), these providing steam to power equipment or provide heating at depots. On 13 April 1990, 52 8012 is seen in steam but connected to pipes at Zittau. The German Class 2-10-0 Kriegslok (War Loco) were built in huge numbers during World War Two to a simplified design that enabled them to be constructed very quickly. This loco was built in 1943 as 52 4944 and then rebuilt in 1961, being renumbered as 52 8012. It was used until 1988 when it was modified to become a mobile steam generator; the loco still survives and is privately owned in Germany.

In West Germany, Deutsche Bundesbahn had invested heavily in the rail network, which was in vastly superior condition than the one DR operated in the DDR. In major cities, new S-Bahn systems involving cross-city tunnels had been built in Munich, Stuttgart and Frankfurt. In Cologne, the creation of the S-Bahn required an extra span for the historic Hohenzollern Bridge over the Rhine. The construction work is visible in this August 1987 view taken from the top of Cologne Cathedral, which also shows one of the short-lived Bundesbahn Class 403 intercity EMUs in Lufthansa livery working a Düsseldorf to Frankfurt Airport 'Lufthansa Airport Express' service. The three Class 403 four-car EMUs were built in 1973 and all withdrawn by 1993. Today, the Class 403 class number has been re-used by DB for one of the ICE 3 train types.

The mainstays of Deutsche Bundesbahn express trains in 1990 were the powerful six-axle Class 103 electric locos, 149 of which were built between 1965-73. On 10 September 1989, 103 148 is seen arriving at Würzburg with Eurocity train EC22 'Johann Strauss' (the 05.58 Köln–Vienna West) in the original red and cream livery shared with Trans-Europ-Express (TEE) rolling stock.

While DR had eliminated steam operation on the main line, it still had eight narrow gauge systems that relied almost entirely on steam locos. The 750mm network south of Oschatz, between Dresden and Leipzig, only had freight trains, all of which were hauled by locos that were between 70 and 100 years old! When pictured on 11 April 1990, Saxon Meyer 0-4-4-0T loco 99 1568 was 80 years old as it passes through Schweta working the 13.15 Oschatz–Kemmlitz freight service with standard gauge wagons carried on transporter wagons. While this line has actually regained the passenger trains it lost in the 1970s, this loco was withdrawn in 1991 and is now active on the rebuilt Pressnitztalbahn heritage line in Saxony.

Most of DR's freight in 1990 was domestic, with exports to neighbouring former communist countries reducing significantly once the DDR started using the Deutschemark as this increased prices for most goods. Romanian-built DR diesel 119 048 is seen arriving at the Czechoslovak border station of Děčín on 16 April 1990 with a southbound freight. Electric operation on the cross-border section began in 1992 and today this route is an important Trans-European corridor with substantial freight traffic.

Three weeks before German re-unification and a rare sight even then as Soviet-built DR locos 120 043 and 132 070 are pictured at Eisenach with a passenger train on 10 September 1990. DR Class 120 was the Soviet 'M62' design sold widely in the Soviet bloc. Passenger use was unusual, although the Class 132 behind was widely used across the DDR. (Jon Hayes)

Chapter 2

Two Countries – Two Systems

At the time Germany was re-unified, its railway industry was dominated by the two separate state-owned railway companies; Deutsche Bundesbahn in the former West Germany and Deutsche Reichsbahn in the former DDR. In addition, there were large amounts of industrial rail operations in both countries. In the east, much of this was associated with heavy industry, although even small factories of many kinds often had one or two diesel shunters. In West Germany, as well as extensive mining and docks systems, non Bundesbahn rail operations were mostly in the hands of small rail companies, often owned by local authorities – sometimes, especially in the south-western state of Baden Württemberg, operating regional passenger services too.

As both the former West German Deutsche Bundesbahn and the unified Deutsche Bahn AG share the same initials, for the purposes of this book DB is used to describe the unified post-1994 company while DR refers to the former East German operator; the pre-1994 West German operator is simply called the Bundesbahn.

Both the Bundesbahn and DR employed large numbers of people (249,000 and 267,000 respectively in early 1990) and most of those employed were treated as civil servants or other central government employees. DR's central role in military logistics, not only for the East German army but also the Soviet Red Army, meant DR employees were regarded as important by the East German state so, to keep close control, there were also substantial numbers of political and security service officials within the organisation.

DR had, like all major organisations in the DDR, been encouraged to maximise employment as the government sought to ensure there was no visible unemployment. This, plus a lack of funds for investment in the 1980s, in part led to the retention of antiquated systems, such as retaining old steam locos to produce steam to heat buildings and power equipment at depots and stations, although it had not prevented DR from closing lines between the 1960s and 1980s due to them costing too much to operate.

DR locos had cast or pressed metal plates, not only for their number but also to show to which depot and division they were allocated. Making and installing these plates created jobs which helped DR maximise employment. The Bundesbahn used transfers and painted information which was much cheaper. The numberplate and allocation plates for shunting loco 105 091 are seen on 11 April 1990.

DR dominated freight transport within the DDR and provided wagonload freight services to every part of the network. On 10 April 1990, 106 464 is seen working a trip freight into Wernigerode from Ilsenburg, then the western limit of the DR as the line to the west had been severed by the inter German border. By 1996, the line through Ilsenburg to Vienenburg in the west would be rebuilt.

When exposed to the new reality of a market economy in the early 1990s, DR was expected to cover its costs at a time when traffic levels were falling dramatically. Cutting many of the most uneconomic activities was quickly identified as a way of reducing costs. In West Germany, change came too but more slowly following the unification of the two railway companies in 1994 and the gradual restructuring of the entire industry.

Varied Locomotive Fleets

Both DR and the Bundesbahn had mixed fleets of diesel and electric locos. Until the 1980s, both were still operating small numbers of the same electric classes inherited from the pre-1945 Reichsbahn. DR also still had many steam locos dating from World War Two in its fleet, although officially main line use of steam ended in the DDR in 1988.

Despite the division of Germany and the fortified border, there was communication between the two railways via international organisations and trade fairs, which led to locomotive development often being similar with, in most cases, DR adopting ideas that the Bundesbahn found to be successful. A common approach, rooted in the pre-1945 period, to classifying locomotives and adoption of similar if not common standards would make the eventual job of re-unifying the two fleets easier. For example, both systems used 15kV AC overhead electrification, although DR did trial the use of 25kV AC as well.

The locomotive numbering systems were also similar, using six digit numbers and a check digit for use in computer systems. However, while the Bundesbahn numbered its electric locos in the '1xx' series, DR used '2xx' class numbers, and for diesel locos the approach was the exact opposite!

DR retained steam locos as Dampfspender steam generators. These were still capable of moving under their own power as they were normally taken back from the steam pipe apparatus to the shed for maintenance. DR former heavy freight 2-10-0 44 1614 is shown receiving attention at Leipzig Engelsdorf shed on 29 March 1991. This loco still exists and is currently preserved at the railway museum at Ampflwang in Austria.

The 292-strong Class 242 locos were the first large electric loco class delivered to DR. Freshly painted in DR's Bordeaux Red livery, 242 107 is seen at Leipzig Hbf on 29 March 1991.

In 1990, DR had a fleet dominated by diesel locos with the most powerful and numerous being Soviet-built locos. The DR Class 120 (DB 220) Co-Co locos built to the 'M62' design, first sold to Hungary and later produced in large numbers for the USSR, were known to DR employees as Taigatrommel. Meaning Russian steppe (Taiga) and drums (Trommel), this referred to their engine noise, but as the class consumed large amounts of fuel and oil, they were destined for early withdrawal after re-unification. The larger fleet of 873 Class 130/131/132 and 142 Co-Cos were derived from the Soviet TE109 design and were more successful, with some remaining in service today.

Mid-power diesels were represented by domestically built Class 118 (later DB 228) four and six axle diesel-hydraulic designs dating from 1960, along with 200 more modern but less successful Romanian-built Class 119 Co-Cos, many of which were stored by 1990 but which would be reinstated later in the decade. Completing the extensive diesel fleet were hundreds of East German-built B-B V100 diesel hydraulics (DR 110-114, later DB 201-204/298) and 0-8-0 diesel shunters (Classes 105/106, later DB 345/346).

By 1990, large numbers of new DR Class 243 (later DB 143) Bo-Bo electric locos built by Lokomotivbau-Elektrotechnische Werke (LEW), the pre-war AEG factory at Hennigsdorf to the north of Berlin, had entered service. The last of 647 locos, DR 243 659 (later DB 143 659) was delivered on 17 December 1990, two months after re-unification.

Main line electrification had been prioritised in the 1980s due to rising oil prices and the fact that electricity could be generated cheaply by burning lignite (brown coal) which the DDR had huge reserves of. By 1990, around half of all DR operated trains were electric. DR also had a large fleet of its first electric design, the Class 211/242 (later DB 109/142) with 388 built in total between 1961–76, along with 273 of the newer (1973–84) six-axle Class 250 (later DB 155) mixed traffic design.

An example of the V100 design, 114 246 is seen at Halberstadt on 13 April 1991 with the 08.05 Magdeburg to Thale service. While outwardly very similar to the majority of the DR V100s, the DR Class 114 (later DB 204) were rebuilt examples with a more powerful 1029kW engine.

DR's newest electric locos in 1990 were the Class 243, later DB Class 143. Just three months old following delivery on 10 January, 243 558 passes Oschatz on 11 April 1990 with a Dresden–Frankfurt am Main D train.

The Bundesbahn's newest electric locos in 1990 were the Class 120. On 25 August 1989, 120 117 pauses at Hannover Hbf with a Hamburg to Munich Intercity train, carrying the as-delivered and then new DB Orient Red livery with a white 'bib' on the loco front. Two years later, these trains would be replaced by the first ICE high-speed trains. 120 117 was converted to a push-pull regional loco (as 120 206) in 2010 and used for around eight years based in Aachen.

The Bundesbahn fleet was also mainly standardised on large numbers of the same locos and, with much more electrification in West Germany by 1990, many of them were electric. Big batches of Einheitslok (Standard Loco) had been built since the 1950s, resulting in large fleets of four-axle Class 110/139/140 locos that shared many components. These, along with more modern Class 111 and less powerful Class 141, worked most passenger trains and freight.

Two types of heavier six-axle locos were also in the fleet, Class 150 dating from 1957 and the more modern Class 151 built in 1972–78. Express passenger trains were hauled by the six-axle 7,440kW 200km/h Class 103 machines and by 1990, all 65 of the latest express passenger locos, Class 120, had been delivered.

The Bundesbahn had large numbers of six-axle heavy freight locos. The older version was Class 150 as built between 1957 and 1973. On 2 April 1999, 150 148 is seen in the old green livery once widely used by the Bundesbahn as it approaches Ulm with an eastbound freight.

The Bundesbahn also had a large fleet of diesel-hydraulic locos. While the iconic V200 fleet had been retired by 1984, large numbers of V160 Class 215-218 B-B locos were in use in 1990, as were over 300 V100 Class 211-213 locos.

While both railways also had smaller numbers of specialist or prototype locos, neither had extensive fleets of EMUs outside of the established third rail-powered big city S-Bahn systems in Berlin plus Hamburg and the newly developed S-Bahn systems in western cities such as Munich, Frankfurt and Stuttgart, which employed the 1970s designed Class 420 EMU.

The Bundesbahn had begun introducing DMUs to replace locos in the 1970s and by 1990, it was introducing large numbers of the new Class 628 DMU while DR had a large fleet of two-axle Ferkeltaxi railbuses to operate lightly used lines.

The mixed traffic green Bundesbahn livery was also applied to large numbers of Class 140 and 141 locos. Green 141 115 arrives at Frankfurt Hbf on 26 August 1995 with a rake of silver regional coaches. Later in the 1990s, these vehicles were given a painted livery rather than polished steel. A handful remain in use in 2020 with DB, although large numbers are used by private operators for charter or additional services.

The most modern of the Bundesbahn V160 diesel types was Class 218 (built 1968 to 1979), most of which carried the then standard blue and ivory livery, which was also used on many electric locos. Mostly used to work passenger trains, Class 218 would head east in substantial numbers to replace DR locos after re-unification. On 15 June 1997, 218 255 arrives at Goslar with the 15.45 Bad Harzburg to Soltau via Hannover.

Some DR Class 118 locos survived long enough to be renumbered as Class 228. Still operated by DR when this picture of 228 736 was taken at Rennsteig on 9 July 1992, it was working in top and tail mode with 228 780 on the other end of the two-coach articulated DR double deck train, this forming an Ilmenau to Thomasmühle shuttle service. Unlike the Bundesbahn, which had none, DR operated large numbers of double deck or Dosto coaches, these being built at the former WUMAG plant in Görlitz which had developed them prior to World War Two. After 1990, some DR Dosto coaches moved west and the new DB ordered large numbers of new modern versions. (Andrew Garrett)

The Bundesbahn had two types of similar V100 diesel locos. The older Class 211 built from 1958–63 were already partly withdrawn by 1990 and all remaining examples, which were concentrated in Bavaria, would be gone by 2001. The locos carried a red livery when new, but most later received an all over blue scheme. Blue and ivory liveried 211 045 was recorded at Hilpolstein on 31 March 1998 on arrival with the 10.11 service from Roth.

The Bundesbahn had invested in DMUs in the 1970s and 1980s. The two most modern types are seen side by side in Vienenburg on 14 June 1997; on the left is 614 078 dating from the mid-1970s while 628 590 was at that time only around two years old. DB withdrew the last Class 614 in 2010, although some were sold for further use in Romania and Poland. Many of the large Class 628 fleet had been withdrawn by 2020, although they are widely used second-hand in eastern Europe.

The Bundesbahn had invested heavily in the urban S-Bahn systems in West Germany. The Hamburg system received 62 new Class 472 EMUs between 1974 and 1984; these are now being replaced by new trains and all should be withdrawn by 2023. One of the sets, 472 040, plus older 470 105 and both in the ivory and blue livery, are seen approaching Hamburg Hauptbahnhof on 12 May 1999 with a S31 Altona–Harburg service.

Chapter 3

1994 – One National Railway

T he process of re-unification for Germany's railways started the day after the Berlin Wall had opened on 9 November 1989 as multiple special trains were provided by DR with Bundesbahn assistance to take East German citizens to West Germany to enjoy their new freedom to travel. Hundreds of special trains operated in late 1989 between the two countries.

Following the rapid political developments leading to re-unification of the two countries in 1989–90, co-operation between the two railways led to practical steps to introduce a common numbering system for locomotives and multiple units from May 1991 when the first all Germany timetable since 1945 was published, albeit by DR and the Bundesbahn jointly. Plans to re-open lines closed by the inner German border since the 1960s were developed and obstacles to interchange between S-Bahn lines at the former border station at Berlin Friedrichstrasse were removed.

DR began leasing its modern Class 243 electric locos, which were still being built in October 1990, to the Bundesbahn before the actual re-unification day, one was also leased to a Swiss operator for five years. By the early 1990s, many of the fleet had moved west with 150 being used for freight, mainly in the Ruhr, and many others eventually replaced older Bundesbahn Class 141 and 139 locos.

In their place in the former DDR, 139 brand new Class 212 (later DB 112) locos, an improved version of the Class 243, were built at Hennigsdorf for DR. This was partly as an economic stimulus project to keep the former LEW plant open, which had by now returned to AEG ownership.

New owner; despite being owned by DB for five years, ex DR diesel 219 112 still showed evidence of its former owner when seen on 6 June 1999.

New National Operator

The new German government decided that widespread reform of the railway industry was needed. Both the Bundesbahn and DR were loss making and needed substantial subsidy simply to continue operating, while with two national railway companies, there was substantial duplication of administrative and management tasks. In early 1990, the Bundesbahn had fewer employees than DR for a network twice as large and, by 1993, 102,000 of the former 267,000 DR jobs had been eliminated.

DR had seen its freight volumes collapse as industrial companies in the former DDR contracted and freight to neighbouring former socialist states dwindled. Rail freight volumes fell from 350 million tonnes or 60.4 billion tonne/km in the DDR in 1988 (representing around 35% of all freight transport in the country) when the equivalent figure for West Germany was 299 million tonnes to just 337 million tonnes for the unified country in 1994.

Rebuilding the country's east–west connections would be a key task for the next decades and to manage this, whilst reducing overall costs, the government proposed that the railway operators be merged. The new railway operator, to be called Deutsche Bahn (DB), would be a company owned by the government rather than part of the civil service.

DB was required to re-structure itself to split train operation from management of the rail network and from 1999, it created five railway operating businesses, each of which was a separate company. Two of these managed the rail network and stations while the other three operated trains, DB Reise & Touristik (now called DB Fernverkehr) ran long distance trains, DB Regio operated regional trains and buses, and rail freight was managed by DB Cargo. With the creation of separate businesses, DB's loco fleet was divided up amongst the new operating companies in 1999–2000, leading to the end of mixed traffic use for almost all the locos.

DR 106 479 at Eisenach on 29 March 1991 with freight for the Opel car plant, which was established at the former VEB Automobilwerk Eisenach Wartburg factory in early 1990 (owned pre-1945 by BMW). This was a relatively rare example of a major East German manufacturer continuing production immediately after 1990, which was achieved by switching production to western Opel models.

Bahnreform Restructures Industry

Legislation to create the new DB and to establish a new railway market framework, based in part on new European laws, was passed in December 1993 and the new DB, based in Berlin, officially started operating on 1 January 1994. The Bahnreform (rail reform) as it was known moved responsibility for funding regional services to the country's 16 federal states (or Länder) from 1996 onwards with the central government providing the Länder with substantial funding to support socially necessary rail (plus bus and tram) services.

However, the individual states made the final decisions on which routes had what level of service. The federal states initially were permitted to award contracts to the new DB or to tender operation of services, or to do both. DB was permitted to run any passenger services that would make a profit, which in practice was the long distance network.

The Bahnreform also introduced open-access operation to Germany, this permitting any licensed operator to run freight or long distance passenger services on the state railway's network in return for paying track access charges. This led to multiple new freight operators entering the market and many existing small or regional operators branching out into long distance services.

Re-unification for the Rail Network

In 1991, an ambitious plan to re-unify the country's transport system by reviving or creating new links between the former East and West German network of roads, railways and waterways was formally established.

Called the Verkehrsprojekt Deutsche Einheit (VDE or Transport Project German Unity), it was split into 17 projects , nine of which were for railways (numbered VDE 1-9) and most of which were completed by 2006. The remaining eight projects consisted of seven for motorway construction and one for rebuilding inland waterway connections. DR and the Bundesbahn were responsible for much of the early planning before the creation of the new DB in 1994.

In its first decade in existence, DB expanded the high-speed network, built the new Berlin Hauptbahnhof station and introduced hundreds of new trains to replace older ones, often moving ex Bundesbahn locos to the former DR territory with Class 218 diesel hydraulic locos being used to displace former DR diesel types. Large numbers of Class 143 electric locos moved in the other direction to the west of the country to replace older Bundesbahn locos.

A long way from the former DDR, 143 328 in the DR Bordeaux red livery was near the Swiss border at Zell im Wiesental on 25 May 1999 after arriving with RB17324, the 08.49 ex Basel Badische Bf.

From 1996–99, DB took delivery of 145 Class 101 6,400kW, 220km/h express passenger locos built by Adtranz. These replaced older Bundesbahn Class 103 and 111 locos on long distance passenger trains and were soon seen all over Germany, as well as working far into neighbouring Austria. The 220km/h top speed was reduced to 200km/h for most locos from 2014. On 25 May 1999, 101 016 is seen arriving at its destination, Basel Badische Bf with IC503, the 05.30 from Wiesbaden.

With the debut of Class 101, DB also introduced widespread use of driving trailers for long distance services from 1995 onwards, this avoiding the need for locomotives to change ends at terminus or reversal stations. In the original red and white Intercity livery, one of the 220km/h driving trailers stands at Nuremberg Hbf on 18 August 1998 while operating IC805, the 09.44 Kiel–Munich, with 101 042 as the locomotive on the other end. This train reversed in Nuremberg to take the route via Augsburg to Munich.

DB moved large numbers of Class 218 diesel locos to the east of the country where they replaced ex DR diesels. On the evening of 29 May 1999, two Class 218 locos, 218 242 and 218 104, are flanked on either side by an ex DR loco at Aschersleben with 232 645 on left and 232 592 on the right. The latter is still in the original DR livery and was working the 17.20 Halle to Halberstadt service.

DB decided to repair and use many of the Romanian-built Class 219 diesels it inherited from DR. Some were completely rebuilt between 1992 and 1993 by Krupp with two new MTU 12V396 engines, these becoming Class 229 which were then initially used for long distance Intercity or Interregio services. On 22 May 1999, 229 170 stands at Zeitz with IR2583, the 09.36 Wilhelmshaven–Gera, while on the left is 219 063 with the 16.07 Gera–Leipzig service.

In Berlin, DB introduced 500 new S-Bahn trains between 1996 and 2004 to replace most of the existing fleet, some of which dated from the late 1920s. Trains built for the 1936 Berlin Olympic Games were finally withdrawn in 2003! DB also introduced large numbers of new DMUs, including several types of tilt equipped units.

DB Expands Internationally

In the 21st century, DB also expanded internationally, both by operating trains in neighbouring countries and by acquisition, buying global logistics company Stinnes-Schenker in 2002 (now known as DB Schenker) and multiple rail freight companies, such as UK rail freight operator EWS in 2007 and Polish rail freight company PCC Rail two years later. In 2010, DB bought UK based pan-European passenger rail and bus operator Arriva. Plans to part privatise the train operating parts of DB itself were announced in 2006 but formally abandoned after the 2008–09 global financial crisis.

Berlin's S-Bahn system had been a victim of the city's division, originally operated by DR but shunned by West Berliners after the Berlin Wall was built. West Berlin-based Berliner Verkehrsbetriebe (BVG) took over the operation in the West in 1984 after which passengers started using it again, although little was spent on renewing the fleet, most of which dated from the 1920s or early 1930s! Trains operated to the DDR Friedrichstrasse border station, although they changed drivers at Lehrter Stadtbahnhof so that the last kilometre was driven by DR staff. BVG handed over S-Bahn operation to DB in 1994. BVG-operated 275 559, built around 1930, is seen at Berlin Wannsee on 25 August 1989 with a service to Friedrichstrasse.

The new Berlin S-Bahn fleet of Class 481/482 trains was delivered between 1996 and 2004. A then new train, in the original largely cream livery, and led by 481 159 stands at Berlin Ostbahnhof on 24 May 1999 while working the 20.20 Potsdam–Ahrensfelde S7 service. Services between Potsdam and Wannsee were only restored in 1992 after re-unification.

DB eventually ordered many tilting trains, mostly DMUs but also ICE units, all using the Pendolino technology produced by Fiat Ferroviaria. 20 two-car units were built in 1991–92 and used in Bavaria, these being withdrawn in 2014 after around 25 years in use, partly due to a shortage of spare parts but also because more modern tilt equipped DMUs were available. Two sets have been preserved, but the rest were scrapped in 2019. Class leader 610 001 was recorded at Nuremberg Hbf in the 1990s mint green and grey DB Regio livery on 31 August 1998 after arriving with the 08.10 service from Bayreuth.

Perhaps the strangest new trains bought be DB were the seven Class 670 double deck single-car DMUs. These were built by Deutsche Waggonbau at Halle Ammendorf between 1994 and 1996 and used for branchline services in the Mosel Valley in western Germany along with parts of the former DDR. They were not a great success and most were out of use by 2001. 670 002, seen at Stendal on 19 May 2000 with the 19.06 service to Tangermünde, was the last to remain in use with DB until 2003. All seven trains survive, some are used by private operators for excursion or seasonal trains.

Chapter 4

Lines Re-open and Close

As soon as the prohibition on travel to West Germany was lifted on 9 November 1989, East Germans started travelling there in huge numbers, most as visitors rather than moving permanently. Both DR and the Bundesbahn started to plan the re-opening of the many lines closed in 1961 or earlier by the construction of the inner German border. Some lines, although severed by the border, still existed on both sides and therefore could be re-opened relatively quickly once the border installations (which in places included minefields) were removed.

Over 20 lines over the former border were identified for re-opening, several in the Berlin area where most connections to the west had been severed with the remaining traffic routed through a small number of highly-secure border stations. Some lines both in Berlin and elsewhere re-opened before the country was formally re-unified. For example, the line from Eichenberg to Arenshausen on the route from Kassel to Halle, closed by the Soviet occupation administration in 1945, re-opened on 26 May 1990, while many more lines followed in the next few years.

Elsewhere, lines that had remained open but which had lost their electrification after World War Two were electrified again. The 92km section of the Nuremberg to Leipzig 'Saalebahn' route between Camburg and Probstzella (the former DDR intra German border station) was re-electrified from May 1995, meaning electric trains could now operate between Berlin and Munich for the first time ever. The Nuremberg to Leipzig line had been electrified previously in 1942, but the overhead equipment was removed by the Soviet authorities north of Probstzella in 1946 and sent to the USSR as reparations.

The line from Vienenburg to Ilsenburg was built in the early 1990s to replace a previous line (Vienenburg to Wasserleben) that crossed the inter-German border and closed in 1945. The new line opened on 2 June 1996, enabling through trains from Hannover to Halle for the first time in 51 years. A year after re-opening, ex DR diesel 232 687 is seen at Vienenburg on 15 June 1997 with the Brocken InterRegio service IR2643, the 10.00 Aachen to Leipzig.

Rural Lines Close All Over the Former DDR

In the decade after re-unification, hundreds of kilometres of railway closed in the former DDR, this removing passenger services from multiple but mostly small communities. Before 1990, car ownership in the DDR was very low as relatively few cars were manufactured and many people could not afford them, even if they managed to get on a waiting list to buy one. This changed very quickly with huge numbers of mostly second-hand cars moving east; by 1995 there were 429 cars per 1,000 people in the former DDR, not far behind the former West Germany with 498 per thousand!

The rise in car ownership coupled with people moving from rural areas with poor economic prospects to cities, especially in the west of the country, led to rural rail usage declining dramatically. DR closed some lines in the early 1990s as it sought to gain control of its finances, which were in free-fall thanks to the loss of so much freight traffic. By 1996, the Länder in the former DDR were responsible for deciding which lines would be retained and, faced with hard choices, the least used lines were closed with most gone by 2002. Ironically, in western Germany, an alternate trend was establishing itself, namely re-opening regional and rural lines closed between the 1960s and 1980s.

Still in its DR red livery, Ferkeltaxi 772 130 was at Deuben (bei Zeitz) on 22 May 1999 with RB 16494, the 20.01 service to Grosskorbetha, with nobody on board apart from the traincrew. Passenger services on this line ceased along with many others in the local area on 29 May 1999.

Even lines assigned modern trains could be closed. DB DMU 928 235 stands at Aken (bei Elbe) on arrival from Köthen on 23 May 1999. This 12.5km branchline was modernised in 2003–04 and worked by even more modern Class 642 DMUs but was closed to passengers on 9 December 2007 as passenger numbers were not sufficient to justify continued funding.

Driving trailer car 972 714 + 772 114 in the 1990s mint green and grey DB Regio livery at Dömitz on 22 April 2000 with the 17.02 service to Ludwigslust. Passenger services on this line ended five weeks later on 27 May 2000.

A busy scene at Güsen, between Brandenburg and Magdeburg, with local people taking a last ride on local trains formed of Class 772 railcars to Jerichow and Ziesar on 24 May 1999. Both lines closed to passenger trains five days later and, apart from a short section of the former Jerichow line retained for freight, have been lifted.

The unique 25kV AC electrified Rübelandbahn line from Blankenburg (Harz) to Königshütte closed to passengers in two stages in 1999 and 2005. Shortly before the line's unique 25kV AC Class 171 locos were replaced by Class 218 diesels, 171 002 is seen with its one-coach train at Blankenburg (Harz) with the 09.51 service to Königshütte on 15 June 1997.

Chapter 5

Traction Transition 1990–2010

Already 56 years old when seen at Berlin Lichtenberg shed on 6 April 1990, this 1934 built two-axle diesel 100 352 would survive until 1998 when DB withdrew it. It is now preserved at the Rheinsberg railway museum north of Berlin.

Both the Bundesbahn and DR had extensive fleets of diesel and electric locos dating from the 1940s–80s and as DB adjusted to the new unified economy, many, especially former DR diesel locos, were withdrawn. DR also still owned large numbers of steam locos, most of the operational ones being narrow gauge; these have almost all survived either in use or in museums.

In 1994, neither the Bundesbahn nor DR had large EMU or DMU fleets, other than for S-Bahn systems in the biggest cities, although the Bundesbahn had begun replacing diesel locos with new DMUs. The move to new multiple units accelerated nationwide over the next decade and hundreds of diesel and later electric locos became surplus.

The decision to swop the old eastern Ostmark for the Deutschmark at a rate of one to one resulted in many industrial companies in the former DDR being unable to compete with those in western Germany or elsewhere in Europe. This combined with the collapse in demand from the former Comecon socialist countries led to a dramatic fall in rail freight volumes in the former DDR between 1989 and 1991.

Diesel Locos

The fall in freight traffic enabled DR to withdraw its less successful diesel locos in large numbers long before the unification of DB and DR took place. The DR Class 120 diesels built by Voroshilovgrad Locomotive Works in Ukraine were the first major type to be side-lined as quickly as possible, with the last withdrawn by 1995 due to their poor fuel economy, although private operators would later reintroduce the type to Germany, mainly using locos bought second-hand in eastern Europe.

In 1990, DR was already scrapping its domestically-built Class 118 (later DB 228) locos dating from 1960–70 and had stored large numbers of the Romanian-built Class 119 (later DB 219 and 229), although many of these were put back into service in the early 1990s.

In original DR livery complete with impractical white roof, renumbered DB 219 119 arrives at Saalfeld on 28 August 1999 with the 14.28 service from Leipzig.

DB decided to introduce new multiple units to replace the widespread use of loco-hauled or push-pull trains across both parts of the now unified Germany. In the former west, this resulted in the withdrawal of large numbers of Class 211/212/213 V100 design locos along with the larger Class 215/216/217/218 V160 types by the mid-2000s. In the former DDR, large numbers of the DR V100 design Class 202/204 locos were withdrawn, either as lines closed or replacement locos and DMUs were drafted in from western Germany. The larger Class 219 locos used for regional trains were all withdrawn by 2004, although a small number remain in use with freight operators in Germany and DB itself uses them for freight in Romania.

By 2000, DB Regio had ceased to use Soviet-built V300 Class 232 or 234 locos in any quantity, although limited planned-use on long distance trains continued until late 2011, working a Eurocity service to and from Szczecin in Poland. Freight operators including DB Cargo continue to use small numbers of Class 232, along with re-engined Class 233, in 2020, although the majority of the once over 700 strong class has been scrapped or sold abroad.

In 1994, DB inherited hundreds of shunting locos, some dating back to the 1930s and 1940s. With the decline in heavy industry and traditional wagonload freight as DB shut hundreds of freight sidings in the decade following 1994, the number of shunters required dropped dramatically. Some were bought by other operators and can now be seen in a wide variety of liveries.

The former Bundesbahn Class 215 diesels were all replaced by modern DMUs by 2003 or so. Unlike Class 218, they were not transferred to the former DDR but spent their entire working lives in the west of the country. In the final DB Verkehrs Rot (Traffic Red) livery, 215 011 arrives at Krefeld on 13 March 1999 with RE8234, the 13.05 Duesseldorf–Kleve.

DB withdrew large numbers of small centre cab four-axle V100 diesel hydraulic locos between 1994 and 2004. One of the last places outside Bavaria where former Bundesbahn 'West V100' Class 212 locos operated was the Pfalz region, west of Mannheim. On 26 May 1999, 212 344 is seen at Pirmasens Hbf with the 11.41 service to Kaiserslautern (RB3573).

In the former DDR, some 'Ost V100' locos received new DB liveries. On 25 April 2000, 202 385 is seen at Sömmerda on arrival with the 18.07 service from Grossheringen with two mint green and grey ex DR coaches. The loco is in the Neu Rot (New Red) livery.

Electric Locos

In 1990, DR retained ten of the pre-World War Two Class E44 Bo-Bo electric locos (as DR Class 244) and a similar number of the largely 1940s-built former E94 Co-Co design. All had been officially withdrawn by the time the DR fleet was renumbered into a common series with DB in the west in January 1992; identical locos in the former Bundesbahn fleet had been withdrawn in the late 1980s.

Large numbers of new electric locos had been built by LEW for DR in the 1980s and these (Class 243, later DB 143 and Class 250, later DB 155) replaced older LEW-built DR Classes 211 (DB 109) and 242 (DB 142) with both types being withdrawn by DB by 1999, although a handful remain in use with private operators.

The Class 143 design, while relatively slow at 120km/h, was ideal for short push-pull operated regional trains and was exported in large numbers, on loan initially, from DR to the Bundesbahn in 1990–93. Once the two companies were unified, the transfers increased and within a few years, Class 143 had replaced large numbers of Class 110 and 111 locos. The resulting cascade of locos, plus the advent of sectorisation and, from 1999, the introduction of large numbers of new EMUs led to the withdrawal of all the Class 141 and ultimately Class 110 fleets, these once numbering over 800 locos between them.

Non-standard DR electric types such as the four Class 156 (DR 252) Co-Co locos built in 1991 were withdrawn relatively quickly by 2003, although all remain in use with DB freight subsidiary Mitteldeutsche Eisenbahn (MEG). The 15 unique 25kV AC Class 171 locos (DR 251) lasted until 2000 when the overhead catenary on their isolated line was switched off; three survive in museums while the rest have been scrapped.

The four Class 156 locos briefly worked passenger trains when new. Still in DR ownership and three months before DB was created, 156 002 is seen at Frankfurt an der Oder on 5 September 1993 after arriving with the 13.54 from Dresden Neustadt. (Andrew Garrett)

The two largest electric classes built by LEW for DR were Classes 242 (DB 142) and 243 (DB 143). 142 261 with the 17.12 service to Falkenberg and 143 345 are shown at Riesa on 27 August 1995.

A handful of older DR electric locos received the DB Neu Rot livery in the late 1990s, including 25kV AC loco 171 009, photographed outside its depot at Blankenburg (Harz) on 15 June 1997.

The Bundesbahn Class E10, later 110, was one of the biggest electric fleets in the country with over 400 locos built between 1956 and 1969, primarily for passenger use. Displaced from long distance trains in the 1980s by Classes 111 and 120, the locos were used widely for regional services until the mid-2000s when they were replaced by new EMUs. In the classic Bundesbahn blue and ivory livery, 110 281 approaches Krefeld on 13 March 1999 with RE3214, the 11.36 Hamm–Aachen.

The small Class 139 sub-class was originally a version of the Bundesbahn's most numerous electric type, the mixed traffic Class 140 which eventually numbered 879 locos built over 16 years from 1957. Renumbered as Class 139 in 1968 to differentiate their electric braking equipment, they ended regular DB service in 2004. Some Class 139s were used for passenger services in Bavaria into the 21st century with 139 312 in Neu Rot livery seen at Kochel on 3 April 1999 on the rear of the 14.41 service to Tutzing. On the left is more modern 111 223.

The introduction of 145 new Class 101 6,400kW Bo-Bo locos to operate long distance services led to the relegation of the iconic Bundesbahn Class 103 Co-Co locos to slower InterRegio services. The withdrawal of most of the InterRegio network, linked to the expansion of ICE services and the removal of all subsidies from long distance traffic, led to the rundown and withdrawal of all but a handful of Class 103 locos by 2002.

DB's other express passenger loco. Class 120, was also displaced by expansion of ICE services. Some were converted to Class 120.2 to operate double deck stock in push-pull mode for DB Regio on the Hamburg–Rostock and Aachen–Siegen lines. By 2010, most of the Class 120s remaining with DB Fernverkehr were largely used for weekend and relief trains or in place of non-available Class 101s.

In the 21st century, the expansion of international high-speed ICE, TGV and Thalys services linking Germany with France and other neighbouring countries led to the withdrawal of dual-voltage Class 181 locos originally built for international use with the last examples withdrawn by DB in 2018. A handful of the locos are now in private use.

The new century also brought the large scale introduction of new Traxx, Eurosprinter and Vectron locos by both DB and multiple private operators. This led to the withdrawal of most of the previous Classes 140, 150 and 151 (ex Bundesbahn) and Class 155 (built as Class 250 for DR) by 2020.

In the 1990s, DB bought large numbers of new air-conditioned double deck coaches. A train of them hauled by 111 183, in the 1980s grey and orange S-Bahn livery, arrives at Fürth (Bayern) Hbf on 31 August 1998 with the 16.23 Nuremberg to Bamberg RE3752 service. By 2020, most of the 227 Class 111 locos built 1974–84 had been withdrawn.

Withdrawal of the Bundesbahn's iconic Class 103 express passenger locos began in 1997 as Class 101 deliveries increased, and by 2003 none were left in service. Relegated to slower InterRegio trains, 103 242 departs Köln Hbf in the snow (with the cathedral in the background) on 22 November 1999 with IR2219, the 08.53 Norddeich Mole–Karlsruhe service.

While relatively new, Class 120 electric locos lost work as a result of the InterRegio network being closed and new high-speed lines opening, in turn releasing Class 101 locos. By 2010, Class 120s were already relatively rare, apart from at weekends when they were regularly used for multiple Friday and Sunday only services. On 21 September 2008, 120 122 passes through Oberwesel with a southbound Intercity service, the loco remaining in service for another decade before withdrawal in 2018. Class 120 operation with DB is due to end in 2020–21, although a small number are now with private operators.

The 25 production Class 181.1 dual voltage (15kV/25kV AC) locos were built in 1974–75 to operate passenger and freight services to neighbouring France and Luxembourg. With the introduction of TGV and ICE services between Paris and German cities, they lost much of their work, although until 2014 they operated intercity services to Luxembourg. In charge of IC351, the 06.24 Luxembourg–Frankfurt, 181 216 passes Oberwesel on 5 May 2003. The last Class 181 with DB was withdrawn in 2018.

The Bundesbahn had 194 Class 150 and 170 Class 151 six-axle heavy freight locos. All Class 150 locos had been withdrawn by 2004 and by 2020, DB Cargo was using very few Class 151 locos, all of those remaining having been sold to leasing company Railpool in 2017. In 1998, both types were still in service as seen at Dillingen (Saar) on 28 November 1998 with 151 118 in its original blue and ivory livery on the left and 150 185 in the Verkehrs Rot DB Cargo livery on right. Class 151s are widely used by private operators whereas all but two Class 150s were scrapped; the two survivors are both owned by the DB Museum.

DR received 273 Class 250 Co-Co electrics from LEW between 1974–84, which became DB Class 155. Used exclusively for freight since around 2000, most have now been withdrawn, although the survivors were sold along with Class 151 to Railpool in 2017 and a small number remain in use with DB Cargo in 2020. On 7 April 2011, 155 248 passes Berlin Schönefeld Flughafen with a ballast working.

Multiple Units and Coaches

The closure of numerous branch and rural regional routes in eastern Germany led to large numbers of the DR Ferkeltaxi railbuses becoming redundant. These had been built by Waggonbau Bautzen between 1957 and 1969 with some being modernised and repainted in DB mint green and grey livery in the 1990s. Many were sold for further use as far afield as Romania and Cuba.

Their West German contemporary, the Schienenbus (Rail Bus), had largely been withdrawn by the mid-1980s following line closures over the previous decade and a half. By 2020, almost all of the DMUs built for the Bundesbahn in the 1970s and 1980s (Classes 614/624/627/628) had also been replaced by new trains, many being sold second-hand to operators in Eastern Europe.

The long distance coaches built in the 1980s and 1990s for DR had a long future; some are still in service in Germany in 2020 and many more have been sold to operators in eastern Europe or further afield. In contrast, the majority of older but modernised DR 'Reko' coaches and articulated double deck sets were withdrawn in the mid-1990s as the lines they were used on closed or they were replaced by either new double deck coaches or stock transferred from western Germany.

DR's more modern double deck coaches dating from the 1970s and 1980s were retained and many eventually ended up in use in the west of the country, some were still in use in 2020. DB decided to buy many more double deck coaches equipped with air-conditioning and these were built at the same Waggonbau Görlitz factory (now owned by Bombardier) that built the earlier vehicles for DR. The factory now also produces double deck EMUs and DB's latest IC2 double deck Intercity push-pull trains.

The Bundesbahn's first DMU class was the Class 624 of which 147 vehicles were built between 1961 and 1968. Used only in western Germany, the last train was withdrawn in 2005, although some were sold for further use in Poland and Romania. A three-car set with 624 637 leading is seen at Osnabrück Hbf on 14 June 1997.

In the late 1990s, many new DMU designs started to appear across Germany. The first Bombardier Talent diesel units built by the former Talbot factory in Aachen featured electric traction motors for use on steeply graded routes. Designated Class 644, they were delivered from 1998. When new, unit 644 011 is seen at Euskirchen on 14 March 1999 with the 13.01 service to Bonn.

Stadler offered a lightweight DMU in the form of its GTW design with a central power unit, which was previously built as an EMU for Swiss operators. Several batches of what became Class 646 were ordered with the first being used around Berlin from 1999 onwards. Two of the first DB batch are seen at Hennigsdorf on 29 August 2003; 646 005 on the left with a Kremmen service and, on the right, 646 028 with RE38258, the 12.02 to Neuruppin West. DB has since sold most of these trains for further use in the Czech Republic.

In 2000, both Hamburg and Berlin still used trains dating from the 1940s or earlier for S-Bahn services. Two Hamburg Class 471 trains are seen in the two liveries they carried at Hamburg Altona on 17 March 1998. Of these, 471 109 in the later blue and ivory livery dated from 1940 while 474 475 next to it and in the original blue livery was part of the post-war batch built in 1954–55. The last Class 471 set was withdrawn in 2001.

The DB Class 476 (ex DR Class 276) Berlin S-Bahn EMU was a 1980s rebuild of older Class 275 trains dating from 1928–31. All were finally withdrawn in 2000, by which time some vehicles were 72 years old! In the last year of operation, a Class 476 train with 476 057 leading is seen at Berlin Ostbahnhof on 24 May 1999 with a S75 Spandau–Wartenberg train.

Chapter 6

High-Speed Network Grows

When new, ICE 1 trains had a white livery with a two-tone red stripe along the bodysides. Two of the sets are seen arriving at Frankfurt Hbf on 26 August 1995 with 103 105, one of the Class 103 express electric locos they eventually replaced, visible on the left.

Germany's first two dedicated high-speed lines, Neubaustrecke (NBS) or New Build Line, were designed in the 1960s and had been under construction since 1973. These opened fully in 1991 with the new ICE 1 trains operating most services. The 327km north to south line between Hannover and Würzburg cut through the hills and valleys of central Germany with multiple tunnels and viaducts, as did the more southerly 100km Mannheim to Stuttgart NBS line. The use of tunnels on high-speed lines was a significant innovation when the lines opened, although it is common globally today. Both new lines, and all those that have followed since, connected existing major stations, thereby avoiding the expense of building new stations.

Re-unification of the country changed the planning for further high-speed lines, which initially had been designed by the Bundesbahn to speed up trains in West Germany. Routes that connected both halves of the country now became a priority as part of the VDE programme described earlier in Chapter 3.

High-Speed Link for Berlin

Prior to the collapse of the East German regime, re-building an existing line across the DDR as a high-speed route for transit traffic to and from West Berlin had been under discussion between the two German governments in the late 1980s. Following re-unification, work began quickly in 1992 and a new 185km-long high-speed route suitable for 250km/h operation opened in September 1998.

Running between Hannover and Berlin Spandau, this was routed alongside the existing, but little used, non-electrified Lehrterbahn route via Wolfsburg, with a by-pass line south of Stendal. The new line not only enabled faster links from the Ruhr and Frankfurt conurbations to Berlin, it also enabled faster journeys from Berlin to Munich, albeit using a very circuitous route via Kassel.

In addition, the existing Berlin to Hamburg main line, which before World War Two had been the fastest line in the country, was completely rebuilt as a 230km/h Ausbaustrecke (ABS) or Rebuilt Line by 2004. Journey times fell from around six hours in 1990 to around 90 minutes today.

The shorter Class 402 ICE 2 sets were built for services to Berlin via the new high-speed line from Hannover. The livery for these was initially the same as ICE 1 with the two-tone Orient Rot red stripes. From 2001, this stripe was changed to the newer Verkehrsrot (traffic red). An ICE 2 led by power car 402 023 passes Ennepetal Gevelsburg, between Hagen and Wuppertal, with a Berlin to Köln service on 10 April 2011.

330km/h Connection to Frankfurt

In 2002, the 177km long and 330km/h Rhein Main NBS connecting Köln and Frankfurt Airport opened. This line, uniquely in Germany, was designed only for use by very powerful high-speed EMUs with significant gradients, although none routinely exceed 300km/h. It mostly follows the A3 Autobahn and has 18 viaducts as well as 30 tunnels, while a loop line serves Köln/Bonn airport and a high-speed branch links the main route to the city of Wiesbaden.

Unlike previous lines, several brand new stations were built, the largest of which is at Frankfurt Airport, where a brand new Fernverkehr (Long Distance) station was built above ground and adjacent to an existing underground regional station. Germany's first parkway-style station was built north of Frankfurt at Limburg Süd, which has been an unexpected success story as DB originally did not want to build it at all!

The Rhein-Main NBS reduced Köln to Frankfurt journey times to around 70 minutes, a significant improvement from the previous best of two hours and 30 minutes via the classic and scenic Rhine Valley route. Since the line opened in 2002, Lufthansa has withdrawn all of its direct flights between Frankfurt and Köln/Bonn and many to Düsseldorf. Instead it 'codeshares' with DB, many ICEs having a 'LH' flight number as well.

Berlin to Munich in Four Hours

The most ambitious of all the re-unification high-speed projects was to create a route from Berlin to the former East German cities of Leipzig and Erfurt, which then connected to Nuremberg and Munich in Bavaria to the south. Built as several separate sections of new and rebuilt line, construction took around 25 years before the full route opened in December 2017, although some of the most ambitious parts of the project, including a freight tunnel under Nuremberg, are not yet under construction.

The central section of the Berlin to Munich route is the 107km long and 300km/h NBS between Erfurt and Ebensfeld, north of Bamberg in Bavaria, which took 21 years to be built through the very hilly and remote Thüringerwald (Thüringen Forest). Construction was eventually completed despite the project being threatened with cancellation on cost grounds from 1999 to 2003.

The line climbs from 200 metres above sea level in Erfurt for around 55km, initially in the open but then in a series of tunnels to a summit at 603 metres above sea level in the middle of the forest. It then descends via yet more tunnels back to around 250 metres above sea level in northern Bavaria.

In total, the line has 22 tunnels and 29 bridges with the central section crossing the Thüringerwald being around 29km long, of which 22.7km is in tunnels with brief gaps between them, these often being on bridges crossing river valleys between the hills. The longest tunnels are the 7.391km Silberberg Tunnel and the 8.314km Blessberg Tunnel.

All German NBS lines are electrified at 15kV AC (16.7Hz) and the early lines were equipped with the LZB cab signaling system to allow high-speed operation. The new lines, starting with the Leipzig to Erfurt route in 2015, have used the European Train Control System (ETCS),

At the northern end, the new line connects with the 123km Leipzig/Halle–Erfurt NBS which opened in December 2015 and features Germany's longest railway bridge, the 8.1km long Saale-Elster-Talbrücke spanning the valley (Tal) of the rivers Saale and Elster. North of Leipzig, the main line to Berlin was rebuilt to 200km/h ABS standards, this opening in 2006 at the same time as Berlin's new Hauptbahnhof station.

An ICE-T Class 411 train is seen crossing the 2.67km long Unstruttalbrücke over the Unstrut Valley on the Leipzig–Erfurt high-speed line. (Deutsche Bahn/Wolfgang Klee)

An ICE 1 leaves the 2,287 metre long Göggelsbuch Tunnel on the Nuremberg to Ingolstadt high-speed line with a southbound train bound for Munich. (Deutsche Bahn/Claus Weber)

At the southern end of the line, the section from Ebensfeld to Nuremburg has been rebuilt as a 230km/h ABS. From Nuremberg southwards, a 77.4km, 300km/h NBS line to Ingolstadt opened in 2006 and from there to Munich the existing line has been completely rebuilt for 200km/h operation. Berlin to Munich (623km) is now possible in just under four hours; before the new line opened in 2017, the best time was over six hours. As a result of the shorter journey times, DB has seen substantial increases in passenger numbers with many people switching from domestic flights.

More High-Speed Lines

The German high-speed network continues to grow, although sometimes slowly as planning permission can take many years to agree for new projects. The next big project to open will be a new 59.5km high-speed line connecting Ulm and Wendlingen, near Stuttgart, which is due for completion in December 2022.

In Stuttgart, the historic terminus station is being replaced by a new underground through station and a 57km network of new tunnels is being built to connect the new high-speed line and many other existing routes. The new station is likely to open in the mid-2020s.

Between Basel in Switzerland and Karslruhe, the entire 191km line is being rebuilt to 250km/h four-track standard and this work is likely to be largely completed by the mid-2030s.

Planning is underway for multiple new sections of high-speed line with construction likely to start in the mid-2020s on new routes connecting Frankfurt and Mannheim, Hanau (near Frankfurt) and Fulda, and between Hannover and Bielefeld. New high-speed lines to neighbouring countries are also planned with a new line north of Lübeck to connect with the Fehmarnbelt Tunnel being built between Germany and Denmark while, in the south of the country, a completely new line is planned connecting Dresden with the Czech capital Prague.

The ICE Train

Germany's Inter City Express or ICE train has become famous around the world and today many versions exist, some faster than others! The first ICE trains, DB Class 401/ICE 1, were developed following extensive research in the 1970s and 1980s. A prototype was built which started testing in 1985 and this was followed by orders for 41 twelve-car ICE 1 280km/h trains, each with two power cars, in 1989; a year later the order was increased by another 19 trains. Introduced from 1991, initially ICE 1 was operated at varying lengths of up to 14 intermediate coaches.

In December 1993, a new design of ICE was ordered, this being a shorter seven-car train with a single power car and a driving trailer; 44 of this new Class 402 or ICE 2 design were procured along with two spare power cars. These trains, introduced from 1996, were designed for services on the new Hannover to Berlin NBS by then under construction. These were the last ICEs with traditional power cars as all the designs that followed would be distributed power EMUs.

In 1997, DB ordered 50 new ICE 3 high-speed trains designed for 330km/h operation on the new Rhein-Main NBS, these consisting of 37 Class 403 15kV AC units and 13 Class 406 four-voltage sets for international workings. These powerful 8,000kW trains had a sleek aerodynamic design and featured a panorama lounge at either end, where passengers could see the track ahead through a glass screen behind the driver. A further 13 Class 403 sets were added to the order and all were in service by 2006.

ICE 3 set 403 025 speeds through Vaihingen (Enz) on the Mannheim to Stuttgart high-speed line on 26 March 2019, leading a second set to give a 16-car formation. Like almost all ICEs, this set is named after a German town or city, not all of which are actually served by the trains, in this case *Ravensburg*. This town is in southern Germany on the Ulm to Lindau line, which does not have ICE services and will not be electrified until 2021.

In late 1997, DB ordered the first of a new slower ICE design, the ICE-T (ICE-Tilt). Designed for a maximum speed of 230km/h, they are able to operate on conventional lines at 20% faster speeds than other trains thanks to a tilt system that employs Pendolino technology supplied by Fiat Ferroviaria. Eventually, 60 Class 411 eight-car and 11 five-car Class 415 trains were delivered. Three have since been sold to Austrian Railways (OBB) but are used in a common pool with DB-owned units.

In addition, 20 four-car 200km/h diesel versions (Class 605) were built, but these proved unreliable and uneconomic to operate so have all been withdrawn. DB next ordered ICEs in 2008 when it purchased 16 Siemens Velaro eight-car 320km/h EMUs. Designated Class 407 and called ICE 3, in the end 17 trains were delivered by 2012, the additional set being compensation for delivery delays.

To begin the replacement of the ICE 1 sets and conventional loco-hauled Intercity trains, DB awarded Siemens a €5 billion contract to build its new 250km/h ICx EMUs in 2011; Siemens sub-contracting much of the body assembly to competitor Bombardier. The order has been altered and expanded several times and these trains, known as DB Class 412 or ICE 4, are being built in three batches, namely 50 12-car, 50 13-car and 37 seven-car sets. First entering service in 2013, all 137 trains should be in use by 2023.

In July 2020, DB ordered 30 more Velaro ICE 3 trains from Siemens at a cost of €1 billion to enter service in 2022–26, with options to buy another 60. Contrary to earlier plans and to support proposals to enhance service frequencies nationwide, all 58 remaining ICE 1 trains will be refurbished for a second time and shortened to nine coaches plus power cars. The 44 ICE 2 trains will also be retained, but DB is likely to withdraw all the five-car Class 415 ICE-T trains between 2024 and 2026.

Tilting into the curve, an ICE-T Class 411 EMU passes Bad Kösen on the classic Saalebahn route between Leipzig and Nuremberg, before the new high-speed line opened, on 26 September 2016 with a Berlin to Munich service.

Class 407 set 701 which, despite its number, was the 17th and last Velaro-D to be delivered to DB on 2 November 2016, is seen weeks later at the Frankfurt Airport/Flughafen ICE station on 13 December. Set 701 is the second Velaro-D train built with this number; the first never entered service with DB but, after testing in Germany, was instead exported to Turkey by Siemens in 2013, it becoming the first of the Turkish Railways (TCDD) Velaro YHT trains.

DB's latest ICE livery includes a green stripe at each end of the train. ICE-T set 411 031 is seen in Vienna at Wien Hauptbahnhof on 8 November 2019 in the revised livery, just before departure to Frankfurt.

Chapter 7

Stations Transformed

As part of the VDE programme of rebuilt and new high-speed lines, several stations have been remodelled or modernised, mostly in the former DDR. The largest project by far was the creation of a new central station for the capital, the Berlin Hauptbahnhof opening in 2006. Built on the existing east-west Stadtbahn cross-city route, this employed massively expanded viaducts with the eastern end of the new station literally where the line used to cross the border between West Berlin and the DDR.

The new station replaced the two platform Lerhter Stadtbahnhof S-Bahn station. In addition to the six-track viaduct station, a completely new set of tunnels have been built to serve a massive underground station with eight platforms at right angles to the Stadtbahn above ground. The station construction work in Berlin, and also Leipzig, was complicated by the high water table where sedimentary rocks, including sand and gravel, can hold lots of water. To construct the underground structures, concrete boxes had to first be built and then these had to be pumped dry as they would fill up with water. Construction of Berlin Hbf involved barges and divers working in the flooded pits that later became the underground platforms!

On several floors between the two platforms, DB has created a major retail centre as stations are exempt from Germany's otherwise rather restrictive shopping hour regulations! The new Hauptbahnhof also has tram and metro (U-Bahn) lines serving it while a new north to south S-Bahn line (S21) is under construction in another set of new tunnels; it should partially open in 2021 and connect the Hauptbahnhof to the Berlin S-Bahn 'Ring' line.

Further south on the new north-south tunnel are new stations at Potsdamer Platz and Berlin Südkreuz while elsewhere in the capital, numerous stations including Berlin Spandau, Berlin Gesundbrunnen and Ostkreuz have been completely rebuilt in the period 2000–20.

The high-level platforms at Berlin Hauptbahnhof are above ground on the east to west Stadtbahn with 143 111 seen on the rear of a Berlin Schönefeld Flughafen to Nauen RB14 service at Berlin Hbf on 7 April 2011. Class 143 locos were replaced around Berlin from 2013 by new EMUs but later staged a comeback due to service frequencies being increased. This lasted until 2020 when new Class 147.0 locos were transferred from Stuttgart to Berlin.

Before the new station was built, DB undertook a complete renovation of the east-west Stadtbahn line across the centre of Berlin. DB Skoda-built dual voltage loco 180 010 is seen on the rebuilt Stadtbahn, approaching Hackescher Markt with the 12.31 Berlin Zoo–Warsaw service on 30 August 2003, which it would work as far as Rzepin in Poland.

The view from the old Lehrter Stadtbahnhof S-Bahn station of the Berlin Hbf construction site on 7 June 1999. The station subsequently closed and was demolished in 2002.

Berlin Hbf is seen under construction on 7 June 1999. The supporting pillars and station box for the underground platforms can be seen while the tunnel south to Potsdamer Platz is under construction in separate pits behind the station box. In the distance, the Reichstag can be seen with the new Chancellery buildings under construction in front of them.

The view from inside the new station from almost exactly the same angle in December 2015. The low-level platforms can be seen while the high-level ones are behind the photographer.

Rebuilt Stations for Leipzig and Erfurt

In Leipzig, a 4km cross-city tunnel with four intermediate stations known as the City Tunnel opened in 2013 at a cost of €960 million. Mainly used by regional trains, the tunnel has removed much of the traffic from Leipzig Hauptbahnhof, which was Germany's largest station with 25 platforms. However, this has not prevented a massive redevelopment of the main station, including a three-level shopping mall.

After the creation of DB in 1994, it was decided to undertake two major station reconstruction projects to evaluate wider plans to incorporate much more retail activity at stations. Köln Hbf and Leipzig Hbf were chosen as, in both cases, large amounts of space existed under the stations to turn into retail space, this having previously been used for other purposes or simply not used at all.

In Köln, this involved opening up the viaduct on which the station is built and adding shops whereas in Leipzig, the €250 million rebuilding project, completed in 1997, involved rooms and cellars under the concourse being excavated. This provided the space for shops with a large part of the concourse removed to provide access.

In Erfurt, which has become a major hub for the ICE high-speed network, almost all of the original 1893 station has been replaced, with just the façade of the old building retained. The rebuild was carried out between 2001 and 2008 in preparation for the opening of the new high-speed lines. A new electronic signal box replaced the 16 mechanical and electro-mechanical boxes that previously controlled the station, while the station itself now has six through platforms along with two bay platforms at each end. The new platforms are topped by a 2,400 square metre steel and glass station roof. The 155 metre long roof also features a 12 metre high glass facade above the original station front.

Leipzig Hbf in 1991 as traincrew exchange paperwork before departing to Chemnitz with DR loco 118 716 from platform 24 on 29 March 1991. Today, the number of platforms in use has been reduced with platform 24 used as an open air museum with several preserved locos, while the adjacent platform 25 is a car park.

The station concourse and retail mall at Leipzig Hbf seen on 21 April 2010.

The most impressive of all the stations on the new Leipzig City Tunnel line is Wilhelm Leuschner Platz, which features backlit glass bricks. A DB operated Talent 2 Class 1442 EMU in the distinctive silver livery used in the Leipzig area is seen in the station on 16 December 2015.

The old Erfurt Hbf had this distinctive and improbably thin signal box, one of no less than 16 different boxes that controlled the station in DR days. This along with almost everything else in this 11 April 1998 picture has been swept away. 143 662 on the right is waiting to leave with the 11.16 service to Magdeburg.

Two decades later, an ICE 1 was recorded at the rebuilt station working one of the first services to use the new high-speed line on 11 December 2017. This had opened the day before, connecting Erfurt with Ebensfeld and Nuremberg. Note the church tower above the ICE; it is visible to the right of the signal box in the 1998 picture.

Chapter 8

International Connections Enhanced

I n the 30 years since re-unification, rail connections between Germany and other countries in Europe have been transformed with new high-speed trains using new lines in multiple countries to significantly reduce journey times. In addition, many international regional routes have gained intensive services or re-opened altogether.

In 1990, DR operated international services to much of the former Comecon bloc as well as services to Denmark and Sweden using train ferries across the Baltic. Direct services to the Soviet Union from Berlin operated daily in 1990, these were also used to convey Soviet Railways sleeping cars from as far west as Paris, Hook of Holland or Ostend.

In West Germany, the Bundesbahn offered international connections to multiple but mostly western European countries with Class 103/111 locos working as far east as Vienna or Jesenice in Yugoslavia (today Slovenia), while locomotives from Belgium worked as far into Germany as Köln or Dortmund and DB Class 181 dual voltage electric locos reached Metz and Strasbourg in France.

Until re-unification, intra German services from the DDR to West Germany (and vice versa) were also international workings, these being operated using DR diesel locos from various West German stations with the East German security services issuing transit visas en route to passengers pre-November 1989.

After unification and the collapse of the Soviet Union, international services began to change with more trains to neighbouring countries such as Poland or Czechoslovakia operating as daytime trains rather than as part of much longer overnight services to, for example, Moscow, Kiev or Budapest.

The main line from Dresden to Prague was not electrified across the border until 1992 but, once this had been done, Škoda-built dual voltage DR Class 230 (DB 180) and the Czech Class 372 equivalents took over freight and passenger traffic. Over the next two decades, services were expanded with regular Eurocity services connecting Prague, Bratislava and Budapest with Berlin, Hamburg and Kiel in northern Germany. From mid-2020, a new Vienna–Prague–Berlin service began operating with a Railjet push-pull set powered by Austrian or Czech Eurosprinter Class 1216 locos.

DR 143 632 stands at Warnemünde, near Rostock, on 7 July 1992 with the 12.45 Copenhagen to Berlin service, which had just been removed from the train ferry just visible in the distance. The train ferry service between Warnemünde and Gedser in Denmark ceased operation in 1995. (Andrew Garrett)

In 2002, DB and Polish operator PKP introduced the Berlin–Warszawa Express service of Eurocity trains with dedicated coaches. For many years, a wide variety of locomotives worked these services, but today they are in the hands of Polish Eurosprinter EU44 locos plus leased modern Vectron locos.

A variety of services have connected Berlin with Moscow since re-unification. Since 2016, these have operated using Russian Railways Talgo-built hotel trains, these being branded Strizh (Swift) in Russian and running twice a week. Russian Railways also operates a weekly Moscow–Paris service via Berlin, this using modern Siemens-built sleeping cars.

As Europe implemented open borders and Germany's eastern neighbouring countries joined the EU, multiple regional lines that crossed national borders, and closed as long ago as 1945, were re-opened and modernised. This process is still on-going with more lines likely to re-open connecting Germany with France, Poland and the Czech Republic by 2030.

International High-Speed Revolution

The opening of multiple high-speed lines in neighbouring countries, plus the rebuilding for higher speeds of lines within Germany, enabled a massive expansion of international high-speed rail services in the late 1990s and early 21st century. The rebuilding of the Köln to Aachen line for 250km/h operation enabled Thalys and ICE trains to use the new high-speed lines built in Belgium to reduce Brussels to Köln journey times from a best of two hours and 43 minutes in 1990 to one hour and 50 minutes in 2020.

In conjunction with the French LGV Est-Européenne high-speed line project connecting Paris and Strasbourg, the lines in Germany from Kehl to Appenweier and between Saarbrücken and Ludwigshafen were rebuilt for up to 200km/h operation, this reducing Frankfurt to Paris journey times from over six hours to around three hours and 30 minutes. For services via LGV Est-Européenne, French Euroduplex double deck TGV trains or DB Class 406 ICE 3M EMUs designed to operate from four voltages were initially used, although DB now only uses the more modern Class 407 ICE 3 trains for Paris services. A daily train pair also connects Frankfurt and Marseilles via Strasbourg and Lyon using the LGV Rhine-Rhône high-speed line that opened in 2011.

Belgian Railways multi-voltage electric loco 1608 speeds through Horrem, between Köln and Aachen, on 14 March 1999 with D428, the 15.14 Köln to Ostend via Brussels. Loco-hauled trains between Brussels and Germany ended in 2002 with the then new Thalys service replacing then. The tracks through Horrem have been completely rebuilt in the last two decades and can now permit 230km/h operation.

French Railways (SNCF) 'InOui' branded Euroduplex TGV 4713 stands at Frankfurt Hbf on 31 October 2019 with one of the longest high-speed services to operate from Germany, the 13.58 TGV 9580 working to Marseilles.

The older Class 406 ICE 3 trains remain in charge of services from Frankfurt to Brussels, although use of Class 407 is planned on this route as well. Class 406 trains are also used to operate services between Frankfurt and Amsterdam, some of which extend south as far as Basel in Switzerland. Dutch Railways (NS) own four of these sets, which inter-work with the DB units.

Services between Germany and Austria have progressively accelerated in the last two decades, largely thanks to substantial investment in Austria to rebuild large parts of the Vienna to Salzburg Westbahn. The opening of the Gotthard Base Tunnel under the Swiss Alps in 2016 was the catalyst for the introduction of daily Frankfurt to Milan direct services. Operated using Swiss Railways (SBB) Pendolino EMUs by DB, SBB and Italian operator Trenitalia, the journey takes seven hours and 50 minutes. This should be reduced in 2021 following the opening of the new Ceneri Base Tunnel, which will further cut travel time on the Zürich–Milan route by a further 30 minutes.

More International Links Planned

By 2028, direct ICE services between Berlin, Hamburg and Copenhagen will be possible thanks to the new Fehmarnbelt Tunnel that is being built under the Baltic Sea between Puttgarden in Germany and Rødby in Denmark. New and upgraded electrified lines are being built in both countries to connect with the new tunnel.

In the shorter term, a revival of overnight trains led by multiple Swedish operators will see regular Stockholm–Berlin/Brussels overnight trains launched in 2021. DB ceased running classic overnight sleeper trains in December 2016, although it continues to assist with the operation of Nightjet services, these being run to and from Germany, partly as replacement overnight trains, by Austrian national operator ÖBB.

The completion of the Brenner Base Tunnel under the Alps between Austria and Italy, also scheduled for 2028, plus new and upgraded lines in those countries and Germany will enable Munich to Verona journey times to be reduced by three hours from five hours and 20 minutes to two hours and 20 minutes. Austrian operator ÖBB has ordered new 230km/h Railjet push-pull trains to operate these services.

A new high-speed line connecting Dresden with Prague is now being planned, but almost all of the German section will be in tunnels, although the line is unlikely to be fully open before 2050!

SBB Pendolino EMU 503 016 passes Offenburg with Eurocity Express (ECE) 151, the 08.01 Frankfurt Hbf–Milan on 14 December 2018. The train is routed via Zürich and then the Gotthard Base Tunnel under the Alps.

The Berlin–Warszawa Express service replaced previous services which did not offer air-conditioned coaches. Before the launch of the new service, DB dual voltage (15kV AC/3kV DC) 180 012 arrives at Berlin Ostbahnhof on 30 May 1999 with a train of PKP non air-conditioned coaches forming Eurocity train EC44 from Warsaw.

During 2018, Polish operator PKP Intercity gave several locos a livery based on the Polish flag to commemorate the centenary of the Polish Republic. PKP Eurosprinter loco EU44 005/370 005 is seen alongside the River Spree in Berlin, near Jannowitzbrücke, with a Berlin–Warsaw service formed entirely of PKP IC coaches on 13 August 2018.

Many regional cross border lines have re-opened between Germany and neighbouring countries in the last 30 years. One of the earliest was the line from Tønder in Denmark to Niebüll, which re-opened in 2001 after a trial operation the previous year. Services were initially operated by Veolia company Connex, although they have since switched to DB subsidiary Arriva. The Connex/Nord Ostsee Bahn single car DMU VT411 operating the service is seen at Tønder on 10 May 2003. The Arriva (ex Danish Railways) DMU opposite forms the connecting service to Esbjerg.

The longest current through operation of locos from neighbouring countries in Germany is by České dráhy (Czech Railway) Vectron MS locos, which run from Prague as far north as Kiel and Hamburg in Germany. ČD 193 297 approaches Hamburg Dammtor on 23 May 2019 with a Eurocity service formed of ČD coaches from Prague.

Chapter 9

Rail Freight Adapts to Globalisation

S ince 1990, rail freight in Germany has changed dramatically with hundreds of operators and a wide variety of old and new locomotives being used. The move to globalisation with manufacturers moving production to lower cost, often Asian, countries, coupled with the enlargement of the EU to include all of Germany's former communist neighbours, plus others such as Bulgaria, Romania and parts of the former Yugoslavia, has changed freight traffic patterns with finished goods being imported, normally in containers. As a result, intermodal traffic has unsurprisingly been the biggest growth area.

Two of Europe's main deep sea ports are in Germany (Hamburg and Bremerhaven) and many of the imported goods for EU customers arrive via these vast facilities, with large amounts being moved onwards by rail. Given Germany's location on the European rail network, much of the container traffic via the other two major competing ports (Rotterdam and Antwerp) ends up travelling through Germany to reach the ports as well. In recent years, the number of containers being moved by rail from China to Europe, where Germany is also the key destination, has grown substantially with around 8,000 trains operating from China to western Europe in 2019.

As in most European countries, traditional heavy industry such as steelmaking has declined in Germany, although several steelworks still remain in operation. Germany has phased out deep coal mining but still needs to import coal for some industrial uses, either by ship from outside Europe or by rail, mostly from neighbouring Poland. Iron ore for steelmaking is imported, mainly to Hamburg from Australia or South America, and carried by rail to steelworks across the country, such as Beddingen (Salzgitter), Eisenhüttenstadt and Dillingen (Saar).

Since the mid-1990s, open access competition on the national network has been permitted and has grown dramatically, although the absolute tonnage moved by rail remains similar in 2020 to that in 1990, this reflecting in part the loss of much traditional heavy coal and ore type traffic and its replacement by lighter container trains.

Many of the early open access freight operators bought former DR locos or similar traction that therefore had approval for use in Germany. Prignitzer Eisenbahn (PEG) owned M62 (DR 120 clone) V200.10 is seen passing Fürth (Bayern) Hbf with a civil engineering train on 27 August 2003. While DB operated this type briefly after 1994 as Class 220, this example was built for Polish Railways (PKP) as ST44 952 and imported to Germany for re-use.

In 2019, total freight moved by rail was 340.5 million tonnes, which was nearly 20% less than the 416 million tonnes carried in the first full year after re-unification in 1991 and represents an overall market share for rail of around 19%; in both France and the UK the equivalent figure would be around 9%. However, the distance travelled by each tonne has increased since 2000, reflecting the large number of longer distance intermodal trains with around 130 million tonne/kms recorded in 2018.

Around a third of all rail freight in Germany today is destined for another country or in transit between other countries. Heavy goods such as coal and mineral ore have fallen from around 30% of total tonne/kms in 2002 to less than 15% in 2018.

Hundreds of Operators

Since the 1994 Bahnreform, hundreds of open access operators have started business with 378 active in mid-2020! Between them, the companies now account for over half of the rail freight market, with 52.8% measured in tonne/kms in 2018. DB, which in 1994 had 95%+ of the market, has lost ground, although it is now investing in new locomotives with the aim of increasing rail's overall share of the freight market from 19.2% in 2018 to 25% by 2030.

Many of the smaller companies operate only a few locomotives and specialise in serving a particular area or industry, while many also run engineering trains for infrastructure contractors. A smaller number of bigger companies have emerged, almost all of which are now wholly or partly owned by state railway operators in other EU countries or major port operators in Germany.

The main ones are SBB International (owned by Swiss national operator SBB), Captrain (formerly known as ITL in Germany, owned by French Railways SNCF), TX Logistik (part of Italian national operator Trenitalia), Lineas (privatised Belgian rail freight company), Rhein Cargo (owned by port operators in the Ruhr region) and Metrans (Czech-based but owned by the Hamburg port operator HHLA). In addition, national operators from neighbouring countries regularly now operate their own modern multi-system electric locos deep into Germany.

Until the late 1990s, the number of locos able, and approved, to operate across national borders was limited. On 8 April 1999, DB 181 214 *Mosel* is seen alongside its namesake river at Wasserbillig in Luxembourg with a freight formed of Swiss wagons.

Ex DR six-axle loco 155 038, in one version of the DB Railion livery, rumbles past Schkeuditz West, between Leipzig and Halle, on 1 October 2010 with a westbound freight. By 2020, almost all of these locos had been withdrawn from DB Cargo service.

DB introduced large numbers of modern four-axle locos in the 1990s for freight services, 15kV AC Eurosprinter 152 100 passes Hamburg Harburg on 17 August 2012 with a train of lime hopper wagons. The loco carries the Railion brand name, which was used by DB between 2003 and 2008.

DB Cargo is currently taking delivery of two types of multi-system locos from both Bombardier (Traxx 3) and Siemens (Vectron MS). Brand new Bombardier Traxx 3 187 185 heads south through Bremen Hbf on 30 October 2019 with empty car transporters from Bremerhaven, these having been used to take cars for export.

Many operators now use the Siemens Vectron locomotive, the company having sold over a thousand of them. Box Express 193 834 heads northwards through Bremen Hbf on 23 May 2019. This loco is equipped and approved for use all the way from Italy to Germany.

One of only 13 Class 264 Voith-built Maxima 40CC locos in existence, 264 001 operated by Stock Transport powers through Regensburg Hbf with an oil train on 11 December 2019. Holding the title of the world's most powerful diesel hydraulic loco, the 3,600kW design was built between 2006 and 2010 and was an attempt to offer an alternative to diesel electric designs such as the Euro 4000 built by Alstom and later Stadler. The market for large new diesel locos is very limited and production ceased after just 13 locos, with Voith ultimately exiting the loco building business altogether.

DB Cargo operates a fleet of Euro Class 66 EMD JT42CWRM locomotives in Germany, which are very similar to the UK Class 66. The German-based machines were initially numbered in the Class 247 series, although previously French-registered but DB-owned locos were numbered as Class 77 in France and all are registered as Class 266 in Germany for their computerised numbers! On 20 March 2014, 247 053 with Euro Cargo Rail branding passes Munich Ost with a westbound chemical train.

Metrans is an intermodal transport operator owned by part-privatised Hamburg port operator Hamburger Hafen und Logistik AG (HHLA). It is now a major rail operator, having bought small Czech open access company Railtrans, which was founded by two Czech train drivers in 2003. Metrans locos are registered in the Czech Republic and it has a fleet of 40 Class 386 Traxx MS locos and 10 newer Class 383 Siemens Vectron MS locos. In addition, the company uses many leased locos. Metrans Traxx 386 004 heads south through Bremen on 30 October 2019.

Several open access operators have bought old electric freight locos from DB. Ex DB 151 017 now in use with HSL is seen passing Gommern, between Rosslau and Magdeburg, on 13 December 2017 with a northbound container train.

Press, which is the main line operating division of heritage rail operator Pressnitztalbahn, has an extensive fleet of ex DB locos, all of which use numbers that refer to when they joined the company's fleet. In the distinctive Press blue livery, 110 043 passes Bremen Hbf on 24 May 2019 with a southbound empty automotive train. This is actually ex DB 110 511 and this number is still used for the signalling system, but it was the 43rd loco to join the Press fleet.

Many of the intermodal trains in Germany are in transit from one country to another. For several years, Italian Railways Class 412 multi-system locos worked freight into Germany, although they have since been replaced by more modern locos. Turkish logistics company MARS has operated trains from Trieste (Italy) to Bettembourg (Luxembourg) since September 2012. The westbound service hauled by Trenitalia locos 412 020 and 412 004 is seen passing Traunstein in Bavaria on 1 August 2013. The HGV semi-trailers on board the train are destined to move by road from Bettembourg to France, Belgium, the Netherlands and the UK.

The eastbound MARS train is seen six years later climbing one of the steepest main line gradients in Germany from Geislingen (Steige) to Amstetten (Württemberg), between Stuttgart and Ulm, on 30 September 2018 with MRCE-owned Traxx AC loco 185 567 in charge.

French-built and owned Alstom Prima locos can be seen all over Germany. Veolia-operated and CB Rail-owned E37517 passes through the vineyards at Pommern in the German Mosel Valley on 2 October 2014 bound for France.

Many neighbouring operators now routinely work into Germany while DB Cargo also does the reverse. Iron ore trains from Rotterdam or Amsterdam docks to German steelworks are now powered throughout by Nuremberg-based Class 189 Eurosprinter multi-system locos. DB Cargo 189 033 and 189 031 make their way through Breda in the Netherlands on 18 February 2020 with an empty westbound train.

Chapter 10

Open Access Expansion

From 1996, each of the 16 German federal states (Länder) took over responsibility for funding local and regional rail services with the Federal government providing funding but allowing decisions on service levels. This included whether to provide new services and re-open lines or to remove services and close existing ones.

Tendering for regional passenger services was permitted but not compulsory and some Länder chose not to, awarding DB large contracts instead. The experience of those Länder that did tender services early on was varied, but in most cases the cost of operation was reduced, even where DB won the tender, and often additional services were provided for no more or less than the previous cost.

In most cases, early tenders were for a single route or local network of routes with operators being paid per kilometre operated. In some cases, the operator retained the passenger revenue, being paid a subsidy for losses, while in other cases, all the revenue was paid to the transport authority responsible for paying the operator.

One of the first new operators to begin services was Prignitzer Eisenbahn GmbH (PEG), which was founded in 1996 and started out operating a rural line from Prignitz to Putlitz, initially as a sub-contractor to DB and later, after winning the contract, on its own. PEG expanded to operate a number of rural lines in north-east Germany, mostly using second-hand ex DB Schienenbus railcars. Later, PEG expanded even further, winning tenders in western Germany in 2002

In 2004, PEG was purchased by UK transport group Arriva, which expanded its activities. In 2010, Arriva was itself bought by DB and as a result, it was required to sell its German businesses, which were acquired by Netinera, this being majority owned by Italian state rail operator Trenitalia.

Several early contracted services were operated using leased modern locos and second-hand ex DB coaches as this was a relatively quick and low cost way to start services. As tendering became more widely established so did the concept of introducing new trains with the new contract, which almost always start on the twice-yearly timetable change date in either June or December.

PEG started its operations using ex Bundesbahn Schienenbus railcars operating rural lines in north-east Germany. Two PEG Scheinebusse are seen at Karow on 22 April 2000 operating services between Güstrow and Neustadt (Dosse). Karow was a five-way junction although by 2020, it had no regular trains at all. The line to Wismar shut in 1998 and has now been partly lifted, while all of the other four had lost regular services by 2020, although summer weekend trains operated funded by the local authorities.

The northern state of Schleswig-Holstein was one of the earliest to tender services and award them to newcomers. One of the initial loco-hauled operations was the Hamburg to Padborg service provided by start-up company Flex Verkehrs AG, which began in December 2002 but ended prematurely in August 2003 with the insolvency of the operator. Another new operator, Nord Ostsee Bahn (NOB), owned by French transport and environment holding company Veolia, took over the contact until December 2005 when DB Regio won a new tender. However, having won another tender, NOB started operating the Hamburg to Westerland (Sylt) line in 2005 for 11 years using a variety of diesel locos.

Another loco-hauled operation started in 2003 from Munich to Obertsdorf operated by long-established Bavarian private operator Regentalbahn via its new Vogtlandbahn passenger subsidiary. This used a fleet of 60 refurbished coaches and new Siemens ER20 diesel locomotives. While this service, branded 'Alex' (Allgäu-Express), has since been re-tendered several times and Regentalbahn is now part of Netinera, the trains had remained loco-hauled. However, from December 2020, brand new Polish-built Pesa Link Class 633 DMUs operated by DB Regio will replace the 'Alex' trains.

Growth of Regional Rolling Stock

As tendering became more widespread, regional governments could see that financial savings of around 25-30% could be made from tendering, with that money then available to fund better timetables, new trains or simply be saved. The biggest single issue preventing new operators, even those backed by international groups such as French company Veolia (now called Transdev) or UK-based Arriva, was the need to provide train fleets which might then only be used for a ten-year contract.

In some cases, leasing firms offered to finance small fleets with obvious re-use potential but, in many cases, DB was the only bidder for contracts as it owned the existing fleets and was able to risk ordering new trains as it could cascade them to another contract after ten years. To overcome this, several of the Länder have established their own rolling stock pools and, in some cases, these now own hundreds of vehicles, locos and multiple units. By owning the trains, the Länder can tender for operation of services and attract a wider range of potential operators.

The transport authorities in the Ruhr region have designed a new fast regional network called Rhein–Ruhr–Express (RRX) and have between them bought a fleet of 82 new Class 462 Desiro 'high capacity' part double deck EMUs, while also agreeing a 32 year maintenance contract for them with their manufacturer Siemens.

The overall value of the contract is €1.7 billion while the first ten-year contracts to operate services with the new RRX trains have been awarded to Abellio (owned by Dutch Railways) and UK firm National Express. A similar approach is planned by the authorities in Berlin to create a fleet of new S-Bahn trains that can then be leased to whichever company is chosen to operate services.

By 2018. DB, which in 1996 ran almost all regional services, was operating around 65% of the 55 billion train/kms operated under contract every year with several hundred separate contracts. In the first decade after the 1994 Bahnreform, the number of train/kms operated under contract rose by nearly 75% from around 30 billion train/kms.

Around 50 contracts are tendered on average every year, both large and small, by 27 different transport authorities. In 2020, the Federal government was providing €9 billion to the Länder to fund local transport, even before increasing this due to the coronavirus pandemic. In all cases, additional funds from local taxation are used as well.

While there are around 65 passenger operators in Germany, several major companies now routinely compete for tenders; the main ones being Netinera (majority owned by Trenitalia), Abellio (owned by Dutch Railways) , Transdev and Keolis (a subsidiary of SNCF) plus GoAhead and National Express based in the UK.

The Bahnreform led to interest in operating regional services from new companies, which also brought demand for new lightweight, cheap to buy and operate trains. One of the early designs was the partly articulated Regiosprinter developed by Siemens Duewag in 1994. In all, 40 of these were built with the first use being in north-western Germany by local company Dürener Kreisbahn (DKB) to operate and re-open branch lines. Most of the Regiosprinter trains have since been withdrawn from use in Germany but remain in use in the Czech Republic and Austria. DKB Regiosprinter 6-009 is shown on 13 March 1999 at Dalheim with a service to Rheydt, which was being operated by DKB as a sub-contractor to DB at the time.

The second lighter weight regional train to be built for the German market was the Regio Shuttle single railcar. Originally designed and built by Adtranz from 1996, production passed to Stadler in 2001 when part of Adtranz was sold following the purchase of Adtranz by Bombardier. The Regio Shuttle can work in multiples of up to five if required and has been widely bought with nearly 500 built between 1996 and 2013. One of the first users for the new trains was the Ortenau-S-Bahn (OSB) subsidiary of regionally-owned operator SWEG, which started using the new trains in May 1998. Two OSB Regio Shuttles led by VT511 are pictured at Offenburg on 25 May 1999 with the 11.34 service to Kehl. From 2003, this service was extended from Kehl to nearby Strasbourg in France using the Regio Shuttle units.

Since the mid-1990s, some train operators have come and gone from the scene. Vectus was established in 2003 with 28 new Alstom Lint DMUs as a subsidiary of two local government-owned rail operators, Hessische Landesbahn and Westerwaldbahn, and won a ten-year contract to operate a 218km long network that included the line from Limburg to Koblenz. When the contract was re-tendered a decade later, Hessische Landesbahn won it directly so Vectus was closed and most of the trains moved to the new contract. The distinctive Vectus livery is seen on Lint 41 DMU 648 163 at Koblenz on 6 June 2008.

New operators in many cases bought new fleets of trains and had to build new depots to maintain them. Eurobahn, originally a joint venture but now wholly owned by French Railways subsidiary Keolis, has been active in Germany since 1998. In 2006, the company won its first contract requiring EMUs and a fleet of 44 Flirt EMUs were leased from UK based leasing company Alpha Trains and built by Stadler in Switzerland. A brand new depot at Hamm Heessen was constructed to maintain the fleet. Keolis Eurobahn ET 5 02 and 5 23 are seen inside their home depot at Hamm on 1 July 2010.

Ostdeutsche Eisenbahn GmbH (ODEG) was the first operator in Germany to use double deck EMUs with 16 four-car Stadler Kiss EMUs in use since December 2012, these operating services from Berlin to several regional cities. ODEG was established in 2002 and is part-owned by Netinera, which is majority owned by Trenitalia, and part-owned by BeNEX, which is a company jointly owned by Hamburg metro operator Hamburg Hochbahn and a UK based investment firm. ODEG has won several new contracts in the Berlin area which begin in 2022 and has ordered 23 new Desiro HC EMUs from Siemens for these services. On 24 May 2019, ODEG Kiss 445 109 approaches Berlin Hbf with a RE2 Cottbus to Wittenberge service.

UK based National Express now has extensive rail operations in the Ruhr region, where its German subsidiary has won several major contracts. The first of these began in 2015 using a fleet of Bombardier Talent 2 EMUs, with 442 371 seen in its distinctive red, white and blue livery at Köln Hbf on 2 March 2020.

The Siemens Desiro High Capacity part double deck EMU has been ordered by many German operators as well as by Israeli Railways. The first Desiro HC fleet to enter service was with RRX in the Ruhr region in December 2018, with set 462 004 seen at Bochum Hbf on 10 April 2019.

The long established 'Alex' Munich to Hof service has used Class 223 Siemens Euro Runner diesel locos since 2002. The service has since been expanded to offer frequent trains from Munich to both Hof and Prague with trains dividing in Schwandorf. Five Siemens Eurosprinter electric locos have also been added to the fleet to remove diesel operation of the Munich to Regensburg part of the route. Alex-liveried 223 061 departs Schwandorf on 11 December 2019 with a train to Prague, which it will operate as far as Plzeň, from where a Czech electric loco will take over.

Services on the Marschbahn route between Hamburg and Westerland (Sylt) were operated by Nord Ostsee Bahn (NOB) from 2005 until 2016. During that time, the regional government obtained a fleet of new Bombardier-built Class 245 Traxx Multi Engine locos, these utilising four smaller diesel engines rather than one large one, enabling operating economies in use. The locos and the dedicated push-pull coaches are owned by a private leasing company but contracted to the Schleswig-Holstein regional government. When the operating contract was re-tendered, NOB lost it to DB, which since December 2016 has used the same locos and coaches, all that has changed visually is the logo on the loco front. In the last days of NOB operation, then new 245 207 passes Morsum with a Hamburg to Westerland train on 31 March 2016.

Tram-Trains in Many Cities

The German city of Karlsruhe was the first to develop the concept of light rail vehicles (LRVs) that could operate on the city tram network as well as on the main line railway, thus connecting outlying towns directly with the city centre. The original Karlsruhe tram-trains were dual voltage electric LRVs that could operate from 750V DC on the city tram system and 15kV AC on the national network.

These were introduced in 1992 and the network has since grown extensively to over 600km, encompassing towns and cities up to 60km away from Karlsruhe. In 1997, the Saarbahn started operating services from the Saarbrucken tram system to Sarreguemines, just over the border in France, using a converted railway.

Other cities have followed the basic Karlsruhe model but added bi-mode LRVs with diesel power-packs for use on non-electrified lines. Kassel was the first major city to do this with a fleet of 28 Alstom RegioCitadis LRVs (ten of which are bi-mode) entering service from 2006. Chemnitz in Saxony has been developing an extensive network of tram-train routes using bi-mode Stadler Citylink LRVs. Smaller tram-train operations exist in Nordhausen (onto the Harz narrow gauge system) and new systems are planned for introduction in Bremen and Frankfurt by the mid-2020s.

The Chemnitz tram-train system in Saxony is still growing with several new lines under construction or planned. The main station was rebuilt with direct connections to allow tram-trains to leave the city network and join the rail network. The bi-mode Stadler Citylink vehicles switch from electric to diesel power in the station. The network is operated by regional government-owned City Bahn Chemnitz with 690 434 seen leaving Chemnitz Hbf with a service to Mittweida on 2 April 2019.

Open Access Competition for DB

The 1994 Bahnreform allowed any operator to run commercial passenger trains but in practice such open-access competition with DB's long distance trains has been limited. In 2001, DB announced that its semi-fast long distance services branded InterRegio (IR) were losing so much money that it would withdraw the entire network by 2004 and many routes ceased from 2002. The last IR route was Chemnitz to Berlin and this ended in 2006.

In 2002, French-owned Veolia company Connex launched services branded InterConnex from Leipzig to Rostock-Warnemünde via Berlin using modernised coaches and leased Traxx electric locos, which in part was a reaction to DB's decision to remove cheaper IR trains. In 2003, the service was briefly extended from Leipzig across the country via Nordhausen, Kassel and Giessen to Neuss in the Ruhr region. While this extension was not successful and only ran between June and October 2003, the core Rostock–Berlin–Leipzig section operated until 2014 when the trains were withdrawn as they were no longer making money.

In 2012, the German subsidiary of American rail investor Railroad Development Corporation (RDC) started open access intercity rail services in Germany, these being branded as HKX (Hamburg Köln Express) and running between Hamburg and Cologne. Despite various changes, including adding a service to Frankfurt, the operation was not profitable.

During 2013, the German long distance bus industry had been liberalised, allowing intercity buses to compete with rail. FlixBus, which was then the country's largest long distance bus operator, started open access rail services in August 2017 by taking over the route of short-lived operator Locomore, which ran services between Stuttgart and Berlin from December 2016 to May 2017.

In late 2017, HKX began co-operating with FlixBus, which offered sales via its existing web platforms. From March 2018, HKX services were rebranded as Flixtrain with Flixmobility organising sales and marketing while RDC remained as the operating partner and provided coaches, train personnel and leased modern locomotives to operate the service. A route connecting Aachen and Berlin was added in 2019.

Flixtrain services initially used leased Class 182 Eurosprinter locos but have since switched to newer Siemens Vectron locos. In Flixtrain green livery, 182 505 arrives at Duisburg Hbf on 13 December 2018 with a Hamburg to Köln service.

In mid-March 2020, Flixtrain stopped all services as a result of the coronavirus pandemic and when they restarted four months later, RDC was no longer involved in their operation due to contractual changes. RDC remains as an open access operator of long distance overnight trains and also operates open access car carrying trains on the line between Niebüll and Westerland, connecting the island of Sylt with the mainland.

A small number of other open access services exist; Thalys high-speed trains between Germany and Brussels/Paris run on this basis in Germany. Meanwhile, French company Transdev operates *Snälltåget* branded overnight services between Sweden and Germany, these using the train ferry between Trelleborg and Sassnitz until 2019. From 2021, the services will operate from Stockholm to Berlin via Copenhagen and Hamburg.

RDC Deutschland has operated a car carrying service on the line between Niebüll and Westerland on the island of Sylt since October 2016, this competing with a long established and lucrative service operated by DB. Sylt is only connected with mainland Germany by rail so all vehicles have to travel there by train. RDC subsidiary Autozug Sylt uses two Siemens-built Class 247 Vectron DE locos to operate services. On 22 May 2019, 247 908 is pictured leaving Niebüll while the competing DB service with two Class 218 locos can be seen on the right.

Chapter 11

Narrow Gauge Survives and Thrives

In 1990, DR still operated eight narrow gauge networks or lines, seven of which had passenger services, and almost entirely using steam locomotives. These lines, using three different gauges, were the survivors of a once much larger series of narrow gauge routes that were mostly built in the late 19th or early 20th century. They had been rationalised since 1945 with some lines rebuilt as standard gauge, while many others were closed and lifted by the DDR authorities.

Most of the lines that survived remained steam operated thanks to the substantial increase in oil prices from 1973 onwards, which made burning locally produced coal much more cost effective. Into the 1980s, steam continued to be retained as the Soviet Union restricted oil exports to the DDR from 1981 onwards.

In West Germany, a wide variety of narrow gauge lines had been severely rationalised between the 1950s and 1970s. By 1994, when DB was created, the only narrow gauge line owned by the Bundesbahn was on the North Sea island of Wangerooge, which remains in DB ownership to this day. Several other preserved or private narrow gauge lines remain in operation in western Germany.

The unique 900mm gauge line from the Baltic resort of Kühlungsborn threads its way along the streets of Bad Doberan to the station, where connections with main line trains can be made. 1932-built 2-8-2T 99 2322 is seen on 9 April 1990; the line still shares the road today despite the greatly increased amount of traffic.

DR had been planning to replace steam locos on the extensive metre gauge Harz Mountain network and ten main line Class 112 (V100) diesel locos had been rebuilt in 1990–92 as six-axle metre gauge locos. Re-unification led to a surge in tourist visitors to the Harz region and the railway soon became a major tourist attraction so the plans to replace steam locos were put on hold. Some of the diesels remain in service.

In DR days, 2-10-2T 99 7238 leaves Gernrode on 9 April 1990 with the 10.15 departure to Stiege. These powerful tank engines were the main loco fleet on the Harz system from the mid-1950s, being delivered from VEB Lokomotivbau Karl Marx Babelsberg (LKM) in 1954–56. All 17 locos still exist on the HSB system, although some have been stored for more than 20 years.

Diesels on the Harz system in April 1991 at Nordhausen Nord shed. Converted V100 199 870 (formerly DR 112 870) keeps company with unique 0-6-0 199 301, this dating from 1966 and which was the prototype for a class of 20 similar 1067mm gauge locos built by LEW for export to Indonesia in 1967. This loco remains on the now privatised HSB system but is stored out of use. Six of the ten Class 199.8 conversions also remain with HSB but four, including 199 870, were withdrawn within three years of conversion to narrow gauge and have since been rebuilt again for use on the main line network.

The Harz system relies on the 1954–56 built fleet of 2-10-2T locos as it did in DR days, especially for the highly popular route from Wernigerode to the top of northern Germany's highest mountain, Brocken. On 18 September 2010, 99 7245 pulls away from Drei Annen Hohne with a service from Brocken to Wernigerode.

Former DR Lines change hands

As part of plans to privatise much of the former state-owned industry in the former DDR, the narrow gauge lines were identified as not core to the new DB so they were slated for privatisation. Their popularity as tourist attractions, and in some cases usage by local people, meant that closing them was not an option, although none of them were fully profitable so a commercial sale was not possible either.

During the period between 1993 and 2004, the eight remaining former DR narrow gauge networks found new owners, which in all cases had backing from the relevant regional or local government. Apart from the Harz system, taken over by the Harzer Schmalspurbahnen (HSB or Harz Narrow Gauge Railways) in 1993 and two lines serving Baltic coast resorts in the northern state of Mecklenberg-Vorpommern, the majority of the lines that survived are in the southern state of Sachsen (Saxony).

While Sachsen now promotes itself globally as a place to see and travel on narrow gauge steam trains, the transition from state railways to new owners was at times fraught with financing problems, this threatening continued operation of some lines. A substantial flood in August 2002 nearly destroyed the Weisseritztalbahn line from Freital-Hainsberg, west of Dresden, to Kurort Kipsdorf. Repairs to the most seriously damaged section took 15 years to complete, in part due to a lack of finance, with reopening occurring on 17 June 2017.

The most southerly of all the former DR lines is the 750mm gauge line from Cranzahl to Kurort Oberwiesenthal, close to the Czech border. 1952-built 2-10-2T 99 773 is seen arriving over the steel viaduct in Kurort Oberwiesenthal on 2 October 2012 with the 15.15 service from Cranzahl.

Most lines continue to employ the same locos as used in DR days, although the Rügensche Kleinbahn has introduced several additional locos due to a long-running legal dispute over the ownership of the original locos. One such loco is 0-8-0T 99 4011, which was built in the 1930s as No. 7 for the Mansfeld copper mine system, which is now the heritage Mansfelder Bergwerksbahn line in Sachsen Anhalt. In use in Rügen since 2008, the loco is recorded arriving at Putbus on 23 September 2010.

Extensions and Re-openings

Several lines have been extended since 1990 with former standard gauge sections re-gauged or dual gauged. These include Gernrode–Quedlinburg, which was re-gauged by HSB in 2006, and Putbus–Lauterbach Mole on the Rügensche Kleinbahn system on the Baltic island of Rügen, which has been dual 750mm and 1,435mm gauge since 1999.

The Döllnitzbahn (Oschatz–Mügeln) 750mm gauge line has reopened to passengers after services were removed by DR in 1975 and has since reopened the sections from Mügeln to Kemmlitz and Glossen. Until the early 1990s, the line remained in operation carrying standard gauge freight wagons on 750mm 'rollblock' transporter wagons.

Long term operating contracts have been put in place to provide some financial security for the lines, although in some cases the contracted 'socially necessary' services are provided using DMUs or diesel locos. The southern end of the Harz system is shared with bi-mode tram-trains, which also operate as electric trams on the Nordhausen city tram network. With the decline in working steam on railways around the world, eastern Germany is now the only place with daily scheduled steam passenger operation anywhere.

Four Döllnitzbahn Saxon Meyer locos in steam at Mügeln shed on 11 April 1990 at a time when DR was still operating freight. Built by Hartmann in Chemnitz in several batches from 1892 onwards, all the locos in the picture were built in 1909–10 and all survive today, several in working order.

In 2006, the Döllnitzbahn line to Glossen was re-opened. Regular services, mainly operated to carry school children, were introduced and two former Austrian Railways (OBB) Class 2091 diesel-electric locos were used to operate most services, these being re-gauged to 750mm and re-numbered in the 199.0 series. More recently, a second-hand DMU has been bought from Austria to assist. On 14 August 2012, 199 031 is seen at Glossen; this historic loco was built in 1940 and previously used by OBB as number 2091.12.

Lines Resurrected

In the former DDR, railway preservation as an activity independent of DR or state controlled bodies began in 1990 as soon as the old regime and its many restrictions ended. Small groups of enthusiasts or local people discussed recreating some of the narrow gauge lines that had closed in the previous 30 years.

Several projects have made significant progress in the last 30 years with the Pressnitztalbahn in the Erzgebirge (Ore Mountains) in Sachsen the first to re-open a significant section of line (8km from Jöhstadt to Steinbach) in sections from 1993 onwards and completed by 2000.

The entire 24km Pressnitztalbahn from Wolkenstein to Jöhstadt was the last narrow gauge line closed and lifted by DR. The last trains ran in 1986 and the track had all been lifted by 1989, a year before the preservation effort began. The Pressnitztalbahn currently does not plan to extend its line any further but has in the last 20 years become a main line freight and charter train operator called Press. Owning an extensive fleet of both old and modern locomotives, it also operates the 750mm system on the Baltic island of Rügen under contract to the local authorities.

In northern Germany, the 9km long Pollo 750mm gauge line connecting Lindenberg and Mesendorf, south of the town of Pritzwalk, re-opened fully in 2007. Unlike the Pressnitztalbahn, the Pollo was part of a much bigger system that opened just before World War One. Once 102km long, it had all closed by 1971, being lifted quickly afterwards.

In both cases, lines that had closed and been lifted were rebuilt by volunteers and now partly operate with restored vehicles previously used on the lines, these being rescued and rebuilt after years serving as storage huts or chicken coops in local back gardens.

Several other smaller heritage lines now exist, these rebuilding short sections of former DR routes or industrial narrow gauge lines in the former DDR, along with former Pioneer Railways, which were previously used to train children enrolled in communist youth organisations about railway operations in parks in several cities.

The 'Pollo' line in Brandenburg currently relies on borrowed steam traction alongside its diesel fleet. For the 2018 season, the line operated steam for several months to celebrate the 25th anniversary of the project. Seen at Lindenberg on 15 September 2018, this 0-6-0 tender loco, 99 4652, was built during World War Two by Henschel (25983 of 1941) for use by the military. After the war, it was taken into DR stock and used on the now closed Jüterbog–Luckenwalder system, ending up on the Rügen line by 1965. Withdrawn in 1969, it was sold to a West German buyer who re-gauged it to 600mm. After extensive restoration, it resumed operation as a 750mm loco in Rügen in 2015.

Meyer 0-4-4-0T 99 1568, which in 1990 was still hauling freight trains on the Oschatz system (see picture on page 10), was working on the Pressnitztalbahn north of Schmalzgrube on 3 October 2012.

Chapter 12

Towards Deutschland Takt

I n 2018, the German government announced it wanted to see the country adopt a regular interval timetable, similar to that used in Switzerland since 1982. This is to be introduced nationally by 2030 and will provide a regular frequency on a clock-face timetable, known as Takt in German, and leading to the whole project being called Deutschland Takt 2030.

The overriding aim is to make the rail network easier to use with connections between services timed to optimise journeys and thus encourage a switch to rail instead of driving or flying. Rail journeys account for much lower carbon emissions than the alternatives, while it is hoped that the process will double daily passenger numbers from seven to 14 million. Construction of at least four new high-speed lines have been proposed as a means of adding capacity to the existing network.

The network is getting busier anyway with a record 151 million passengers using long distance rail services in Germany during 2019 according to the German Federal Statistical Office (Destatis), although numbers fell dramatically in 2020 due to the coronavirus pandemic and are not expected to reach 2019 levels again until 2022. Regional rail usage has been increasing annually and has grown by 41.8% since 2004.

Decade to Implement

Full implementation of the plan will take at least a decade with train frequencies of every 30 minutes on routes between major cities and hourly on other routes. Switzerland moved to a half-hourly Takt timetable between major cities as long ago as 2004. DB has put the plan at the centre of its Strong Rail strategy and has suggested that it may need around 120 extra ICE/Intercity trains to achieve the proposed frequency, bringing the total fleet to 600 trains.

It is unclear what role, if any, open access companies will have in operating the future Deutschland Takt long distance trains, although private operators will undoubtedly run much of the regional network that connects with the long distance system.

The first route to get a half-hourly frequency will be Berlin to Hamburg from December 2020 and this will become a test case to establish the impact of additional high-speed trains on both regional and freight traffic.

One of DB's latest ICE 4 trainsets (on the right) stands alongside an original ICE 1 train at Kassel Wilhelmshöhe on 29 February 2020. By 2023, all 58 remaining ICE 1 trains will be refurbished as nine-car sets and all 137 ICE 4 should be in service.

DB has announced orders for some new trains already. In 2019, it bought the entire fleet of 17 Stadler Kiss double deck EMUs used by Austrian open access operator Westbahn and will introduce these between 2020–22 after rebuilding, branded as IC2. DB already has 69 double deck push-pull trains branded IC2 on order from Bombardier, these being powered by a Traxx AC locomotive and which should all be in use by 2022.

The national operator has also ordered 23 17-car trains, known provisionally as ECx, from Spanish manufacturer Talgo to work with multi-system electric locos. These new trainsets will allow the withdrawal of some older Intercity coaches and probably some Class 101 locos as well.

DB has also ordered more ICE trains (137 ICE 4 and 30 Velaro MS ICE 3). To accommodate the large increase in frequencies, it is no longer planning to withdraw either the ICE 1 or ICE 2 fleets. Under earlier plans, both types would have been largely replaced by ICE 4, but instead the ICE 1 and ICE 2 fleets will be rebuilt and used until at least the mid-2030s.

Infrastructure Investment

Substantial investment is required to create capacity for more trains, especially in major cities where congestion already causes delays to the existing network. Some of this is already underway, particularly in Stuttgart where a new underground through station will replace the existing terminus by the mid-2020s with around 30km of new tunnels under the city. A new high-speed line connecting Stuttgart to Ulm will open in 2022.

In late 2019, the German government agreed an €86 billion five-year budget for investment in the country's rail infrastructure, a substantial increase compared to the previous decade. Much of the money will be spent on improving the overall state of repair of the network and adding capacity at congested pinch points to enable the introduction of the planned Deutschland Takt timetable.

In order to operate a true clock face timetable while also speeding up journeys to attract passengers from flying or driving (most German motorways still have no speed limits), several brand new high-speed lines have been identified as required. Construction of some of them is likely to commence in the 2020s following a change in planning law in 2020, this giving the Federal government, rather than multiple local authorities, control of planning approval for certain major national rail or waterway projects.

An artist's impression of the new Talgo ECx trains on order for DB. Danish Railways (DSB) has also ordered eight similar 13-coach 200km/h loco-hauled sets from Talgo to operate international services to Germany, mainly between Hamburg and Copenhagen. (Deutsche Bahn)

New high-speed lines have been proposed which may be built using the new, faster, planning process between Hannover and Bielefeld along with Nuremburg to Würzburg. These are in addition to existing plans for a line connecting Hanau and Fulda, west of Frankfurt, which may include a new underground ICE station beneath the existing Frankfurt Hauptbahnhof and for a new line connecting Frankfurt and Mannheim. Rebuilt or new high-speed lines connecting Hannover with both Bremen and Hamburg plus a rebuilt high-speed Fulda to Erfurt line are also planned.

To shorten journey times, faster speeds are planned on some existing high-speed lines with the Berlin to Hannover route likely to be upgraded to 300km/h. Shorter new sections of line to extend existing routes, especially in urban areas, are also being examined.

Regional Connections

The planned Deutschland Takt timetable will only work effectively if passengers can make seamless journeys using not only long distance trains but also regional ones as well, along with buses or trams. As regional train frequencies and timetables are largely specified by regional governments, there will be a need to co-ordinate the overall timetable to ensure connection times are not too long, thus discouraging use, or too short to threaten reliability.

In many conurbations, regional services already operate on clock-face type schedules so integration with long distance workings is likely to be simple. In the Ruhr region, the new Rhein–Ruhr–Express (RRX) network is also due to commence fully in 2030. Using a mixture of targeted infrastructure/capacity enhancements and a brand new fleet of high performance trains, frequencies will be increased on key routes, thereby offering many more seats to passengers than currently.

More Eco-Friendly Trains

In addition to the new high-speed lines, continued electrification of main lines and regional routes is planned to remove diesel operation and to permit expansion of the long distance network. Specific routes that have been prioritised are Nuremberg/Regensburg to Hof and the Czech border along with Leipzig to Chemnitz. Several major lines in southern Germany (Munich–Lindau and Ulm–Lindau) have been electrified in recent years with electric operation due to start in 2020–21.

The Alstom hydrogen-powered iLint train at its public launch at the Innotrans show in Berlin in 2016.

Thanks to developments in battery and fuel cell technology, electrically-powered regional trains are now appearing in Germany that either do not need overhead wires or can operate without them for extended periods thanks to onboard batteries.

Germany led the world in introducing hydrogen-powered trains in 2018; the Alstom-built iLint being effectively an EMU without overhead power collection and instead has roof-mounted hydrogen fuel cells which feed batteries carried under the train. Special hydrogen fuelling depots are required for the trains, which are now in service west of Bremen, with a further 27 sets planned for use around Frankfurt from 2022.

Several train manufacturers now offer battery power in addition to overhead power for new EMUs and these will become common across Germany by the mid-2020s. In some places, this will remove the need for regional lines to be electrified with overhead wires.

Europe-Wide Takt?

The German government is enthusiastic about introducing the Takt concept across borders to make rail a much more attractive option for passenger transport. Whether this actually happens remains to be seen as, while several of Germany's neighbours already have regular interval timetables as a norm, two of the largest in France and Poland do not. Both the government and the industry also want to increase freight volumes substantially over the next decade as a means of reducing lorry movements and carbon emissions.

Germany's railways have come a long way since 1990 and changed enormously. The Deutschland Takt plan with multiple new lines and new services, much more freight (if it happens) along with new propulsion technologies such as batteries and hydrogen mean that the next few decades will also bring major changes from today.

Above left: The new underground Stuttgart Hauptbahnhof under construction on 13 December 2019, which is likely to open by 2025. The tunnels visible at the western end of the eight-track through station will lead to the lines to Mannheim and Nuremberg.

Above right: A pair of 320km/h ICE 3 Class 407 trains led by 407 005 passes Amstetten (Württemberg) on 30 September 2018 with a service from Munich. From December 2022, ICE trains will no longer need to use the slow and hilly route from Ulm to Stuttgart via Amstetten but instead will traverse the new Wendlingen–Ulm high-speed line.

Glossary

Deutsche Bundesbahn (Bundesbahn) – West German state railway 1949–94.
Deutsche Reichsbahn (DR) – East German state railway 1949–94.
Deutsche Bahn AG (DB) – post-1994 German national rail operator.

Bundesrepublik Deutschland – formal name for West Germany until 1990 and all of Germany since then.
Deutsche Demokratische Republik (DDR) – East Germany/German Democratic Republic.
Council for Mutual Economic Assistance (Comecon) – Eastern bloc pre-1990 trading area.

ABS (Ausbaustrecke) – existing line rebuilt to high-speed standards.
DMU (Diesel Multiple Unit) – self-propelled diesel-powered train.
EMU (Electric Multiple Unit) – self-propelled electrically-powered train.
Hbf (Hauptbahnhof) – main station.
ICE (InterCity Express) – German high-speed train.
LEW (Lokomotivbau-Elektrotechnische Werke) – the main locomotive factory in the DDR, located at the pre-war AEG factory site in Hennigsdorf.
NBS (Neubaustrecke) – new build line or high-speed line.
VDE (Verkehrsprojekt Deutsche Einheit) – Transport Project German Unity, post-1990 programme of new and rebuilt railways, motorways and waterways.